Cool Hard Memories

By Klaus Ahuna

and assisted by Connie Shipley

Written by Klaus Ahuna

Formatted and edited by Connie Shipley

www.CapturingYourLifeStories.com

April, 2019

ISBN: 9781093624755

Dedication

This is dedicated to my mother, Eva Waltraut Klein Ahuna. God Bless you.

Mom passed away December 4, 2018.around 10:00pm. She was 84 years old, but ageless to me. She fought that cancer but, in the end, it took her in her sleep. However, doped up she was forced to be, in order to kill the constant pain, Dad called mom a trooper. Indeed, she was a fighter, but she had no choice but to succumb. It was peaceful, like sleep. Her spirit went to the heavens. I will especially remember Thanksgiving. Mom asked that we all hold hands. I said a short grace for everyone. Dad said a short Hawaiian quote and I finished with an "Amen." That was the first time our immediate family did that for any occasion, a memory I will never soon forget. Thank you, mom, for everything, and anything. Our family will always remember you and love you.

Your oldest son, Klaus.

Contents

Introduction

As I write them, these stories are accurate to me, mostly because I either survived it or lived through it. Some of it is happy times, some sad moments, exciting, and exhilarating times, and some funny excerpts. Some are hell and back stories. There are youthful memories that are as vivid today as when the events occurred. There are memories that will be with me until my final breath on this earth. I hope the reader will get some sense of enjoyment going through my stories, and potentially get from this is a different perspective on life. So now, read this book and voyage through my remembrances.

If it is wisdom you seek,

Deep within yourself you know it.

Experience it.

Klaus Ahuna

My Family

I was born April 15, 1963, in West Berlin, Germany as Klaus George Klein. Later I adopted my Father's name, so I am Klaus George Ahuna. The paperwork was done in the Coos County Courthouse.

My parents met in Germany when my dad was serving in the Army. My mom is a special lady. When I was born in Germany, I was cared for by her, my grandmother Ilse, and my Aunty Johanna. They nurtured me and babied me as babies are treated.

Dad went back to Hawaii after the service. He tried to see if there could be a cohesive life on his side of the family. He discovered not. Dad went to Coos Bay, from Hawaii partly because of urging from Harry Bridges to relocate. So, five Hawaiians did relocate to the area where I was raised. I was two years old when I arrived in Coos Bay from Germany with mom. My sister Kai, and brother Kane were born in Coos Bay.

Mom and dad raised the most complete family. A friend of mine once said, "Your dad is a genius." As kids and now as adults, no one is treated different from the other. We were taught to eat everything on our plates, fix our beds, and keep our rooms

presentable. We were always neat and clean when going to school. Breakfast, lunch, and dinner were always ready. Thank you, Mom!

I'm proud to say that I was raised in the North Bend/Coos Bay area. It is a beautiful place to have been raised. The things that we did, fishing, clamming, crabbing, and so much more. In school, I know

MERRY CHRISTMAS ★ HAPPY NEW YEAR

1967

that I probably would have dropped out but for the sports programs. As a family, we were in love with everything, including the hard rain. The scenery here is breathtaking - the ocean, sea cliffs, light houses, forests, and much more. The dunes are another place to enjoy, with rolling hills, and slopes. The spring and summers are the best times on the southwest Oregon coast. The people here are like no other - friendly. Curry County is also cool with the same weather temperament. All in all, the whole Oregon coast is unlike any other place around.

High School for me was just OK. Yah, there was some fun times, especially with friends, and sports. Other than that, it was doing the curriculum and gathering credits and preparing for graduation. There were some parties along the way. Beer, kegs, pot, guys and gals, it was fun. Usually nobody got too sloshed and everybody had a good time. I never really had a steady girlfriend all through high school but that doesn't mean I didn't like girls, or them me. We had one phone, a land line. If a girl called the whole family would know about it. It happened a few times. I basically ignored it or was just mean over the phone. That was just my way of dealing with the phone.

High school German allowed me to go to seven different countries in Europe solo! My teacher was Hans Lawall. Sports, and athletics were my forte in high school. Without that I probably never would have made it through school. As it turned out, I earned a college degree. That was dad's ultimate goal: to see his kids get a quality education. Mom and dad did all the things necessary to see that through. Through hard work and perseverance, we all were college educated.

Grandfather

My Hawaiian grandfather Wallace was a firefighter for a branch of the Hilo Fire Department. He rescued seven men from the hold of a ship that was leaking ammonia. After the rescue, Grandpa got very sick. His hood had a leak in it. He was hit by ammonia poisoning. He waited with family outside a fence; owned by the government. There were special herbs on the other side of the fence. Nobody was allowed in. Grandpa died on the outside of the fence with family by his side. He was 31 years old. Dad was six.

Wallace Ahuna, my grandfather.

Dad

Dad, our main provider, has a fascinating past. He was born in Keaukaha, a village area outside of Hilo on the big island of Hawaii. Dad grew up as "Chiefy". Nobody there knew him as anything else. Dad has always been a provider, be it fish from spear fishing to pork from the mountains, hunting with the uncles, to growing lush, lavish gardens of vegetables. Keaukaha was a rough place to live. This leads me to believe that he had to earn his nickname. Dad and my uncle Walter were part actors in a color movie with a sad ending called "The Bird of Paradise". They were kids. The main actors were Jeff Chandler, Deborah Panget, and Louis Jourdain. Later, dad got drafted by the Army and did his basic training at the Schofield barracks on Oahu. Than he was shipped to Germany. He became a Boxer, mostly to stay out of the cold weather. Eventually he met mom.

A funny quip: When Dad was in the Army. He made a collect call home for some of his own money. My Grandma Edna picked up the phone. The operator asked her if she would accept the charges from George Ahuna. She replied, "There is no George in this family." My uncle Wallace, overhearing the conversation, said to Grandma, "It's Chiefy! Ma, Chiefy!" The call went through.

Yes, there are times when sons and fathers get into arguments. Also, there are times when they get into fights. I don't remember when or what exactly we were fighting about, but dad got so mad that he unloaded a haymaker at me. Fortunately, I saw it coming and ducked it. The punch landed on the kitchen counter. Dad cracked the Formica and did nothing to his hand. Mom jumped in between us, hysterical, and made us stop. There are times even now when I wonder "what if that punch would have landed." Even dad himself said, 'Lucky you were quick.

Mother

My mother, Eva Waltraut Klein, had quite a time of it as a little girl in West Berlin, Germany between 1939 thru 1945 WWII. She experienced the horror of the intense bombing and then the aftermath of the war and the extremely cold winters where my mom, aunt, and Oma (grandmother) had to huddle together for warmth and scrape for food just to stay alive. There was no basics to fall back on. Somehow my Oma managed to get them through all that. After some time, after there had been some reconstruction, mom got a job in a store of some kind - hardware cashier, I believe. Later yet, mom was with her girlfriends at a dance hall. That is where mom

met George Ahuna, a strapping Army Sargent. As a couple, I might add, they are about the best ballroom dancers I know, mesmerizing to watch.

Dad and mom are Bonsai masters, with a nursery of plants, trees, shrubs, etc. Anyone that visits always comments on the

12

Mom and dad were great parents.

beauty of the miniature trees. They have been to numerous shows and have hosted numerous shows. My favorite tree was an Incense cedar, huge for a Bonsai, yet it was potted. One limb was estimated at 100 years old. The tree might have been close to 300 years old. Amazing, something that sized down and trimmed could be that old.

Kai

In this book I have rarely mentioned Kai, my sister. She really had to study hard to keep up good grades. While Kane and I had it easier that way. Kai is now an Ultrasound specialist and can get a job anywhere in the world. Kudo's to Kai for all her effort. We all

The family at Kai's wedding: mom, Kai, myself and dad with Kane in the background.

have work schedules now so almost everything revolves around work.

There was a time when I must have been six years old. Kai and Kane were younger. The family car was an old Falcon. Dad was driving with us kids in the back seat. Back then there was no child protection devices, so we just sat back there, maybe belted in. I don't remember, and don't know for sure. We drove into the gravel driveway by the house. Dad went into the house for something; having us wait for him in the car. After about some 30 seconds when he went into the house, the car mysteriously started rolling. Kai, the smart one at that particular time, said, "Daddy, the car's moving." Dad bolted out of the house, jumping over the balcony, and running us down just as we were going to fall over a cliff near the house. We were very fortunate. We had rose bushes behind a wire fence. That broke the rolling of the car enough for dad to catch us and stop the car.

Kane

I heard it from Mom one day not long ago about when we moved to the new house. Kane was going to the bus stop for school. He was surrounded by some kids his age. They wanted to kick his ass when one of the kids said, "That is Klaus Ahuna's brother." They left him alone. I guess that's what being a big brother is all about.

I have to tell you all this because it really was something to witness. There was a track meet in the spring of 1978 at Marshfield High School's Pirate stadium. Kane was to run in the 660-meter race, one and a half laps. It was the grade school championship. Kane was in the sixth grade. He was so small compared to his competition. Some of those boys had beards starting, already mature. Dad and I were in the stands, along with Larry Mollers. When the race started, Kane was dead last. Dad was upset with this said, "Shit, I'm going back to work." Suddenly Larry stood up and said, "Wait George, he's making his move." Sure enough, Kane took to the outside of the track. He was passing kids. The crowd started getting into it. Kane ended with a sprint and left the leaders like they were standing still. The crowd was in an uproar. Who was this little kid? Larry grabbed dad and hugged him in glee. My friends surrounded me and said, "Your brother is really good." Yes, I was proud of him too. He reminded me of the Olympic 800-meter Champion Dave Wottle. What a race!

One day when we were still quite young, I was taking a bath in our old house. I had just gotten out of the tub and was drying off. The linen closet door was open blocking anybody's view. Suddenly the door flew open and I heard, "HAH!" I turned around and Kane, thinking he was going to kick me in the butt, miscalculated and kicked me in the cajonies. I dropped like a sack of potatoes. Dad heard what happened. He gave Kane a licking he still remembers. Meanwhile, dad was getting me to jump up and down. He said it would make my balls fall back in place.

One day Kane and I were in the downstairs area of the house. I was maybe fourteen years old. Kane and I were practicing circus stunts. I was on my back and shoulders. With my legs in the air, bent to me. Kane was maybe ten years old. He put his ass on my feet. I would propel him in the air. It took a while to reach a continuity. Soon Kane was flying in the air to the other side of the house, landing deftly on his feet. Man, was that fun. We were adding things Kane would do without hitting the ceiling. Suddenly the Langley's came over to the house. Jerry Langley came storming down the stairs. Immediately he began begging us to let him do what Kane was doing. Kane and I tried to prevent that. He wouldn't stop so I gave him his chance. He ended up bouncing off the ceiling, fell flat on the floor, and completely had the wind knocked out of him. Then came the loud incessant crying. That lousy stunt by Jerry played hard on my butt. Dad yelled, "Klaus," from upstairs and gave me a pretty good licking for that.

My home life during my early years was really good in Coos Bay. We were made to go to church early on. I remember being baptized together with a childhood friend, Tim Looney. Tim and I did camps and sports together. Grade school was a rough area for me. Englewood grade school had some tough kids, some of them a couple years older than me and bigger. I matched up with them quite nicely. One day a bully named Mike Bolen, slammed my brother's head on the merry-go-round. I heard about it. I found Mike, tapped him on the shoulder. When he turned around, I hit him with a bomb that sent him spinning. He ran away. Mike and I had go-arounds a few times. Actually, when I was in 8th grade, I got shit-faced drunk. Two other kids were drinking two pints of Mogen David 20/20 rotgut wine. I got the worst of it. I blacked out and was found in the Mingus Park swamp by none other than Mike Bolen. He took me to the swimming pool where he had a job. He called my parents and got me home. Thank you, Mike. I'm grateful!

When Kane and I were young men, about six or seven years of age, dad started us on a program - the infamous pull-ups. Overhand on the pull-up bar, not underhand chin-ups. It was not a friendly competition. We were serious about outdoing each other. You ought to know this. Dad never lost, even if he had to pull it out by one. I was first. Kane was next that little bone butt. We averaged between 16 and 25 pull-ups daily. That was just one session. We sometimes did two sessions in a day. That's when either Mom or

Kai kept count. This regiment lasted until we went off to college; even later. All that did was make us the better athletes around. They gave us the physical strength to pull out most sporting events. Now I don't think that I can even do five good overhand pull-ups. Man, does the time and non-practice of an exercise catch up with you. I, along with Dad and Kane, have pulled up our own body weights many, many times. That was probably one of the best exercises dad had us do. It taught us how to persevere.

Swimming

When we were young, and still kids, the folks had us all taking swim lessons. This led to us being on the swim team, the Gold Coast swim team of Coos Bay, Oregon. Ralph Mohr and Gary Gehlert (deceased) were the main coaches. Kane was the overall best of the three of us, making the finals most of the time. My strength was breaststroke and backstroke. We went all over the state for swim meets. Kai swam too and plugged away. We all did well with swimming.

It was the last day of school my freshman year of high school. My friends David Bebee, Monte Landon, and me were going up the river on the Allegheny side to the infamous swing. It was a bright sunny day. Beer and Pot were around. The summer had just begun. The swing itself was dangerous if you didn't hold on tight. There was a platform, some forty feet up on a big tree. You had to jump out. There would be a straight drop of about 10'-15'. Like I said, you had to hold on tight to the bar on the rope. At the end of the drop; the swing would catch and carry you over the water. Back and forth. Needless to say, I had to try some funky stunt. I thought that if I let go when the swing was at its highest apex over the water I could let go and do a back flip into the water. I let go when the apex was at about 15'. I lost my balance and landed on my side. When I came out of the water, I couldn't hear anything out of my right ear. When I got home, I tried ear drops and lost all equilibrium. The next day dad took me to an ear specialist. The doctor looked in my ear and said, "Jesus Christ." Then dad looked. I had blown out my eardrum! The doctor did repair work. He put a piece of paper over the hole. I could hear again. Eventually a new eardrum grew over the paper. The swing no longer exists. A girl got seriously hurt. She is now a paraplegic.

Kai and Kane went into lifeguarding after high school. I did as well, for a summer at Black Butte ranch, lifeguarding and teaching swim lessons. In my off-time I dove for golf balls in the icy mountain ponds on the greens. When I dove for balls 18" to 20" rainbow trout were all around. I sold the balls for 25 cents a ball to the golf pro and the golf shop. The three of us are one with the water, just like most Hawaiians.

Piano Lessons

For some two to three years. Kai, Kane, and I were to practice piano lessons. I guess it was so we would be musically inclined. An elderly lady, Mrs. Cox, started us out with middle C, the center. To be quite honest, that's all I know now. We all had half hour lessons once a week. If we didn't hit the right key Mrs. Cox made sure we did it right by rapping us across our fingers with a stick. A few of those and you would never forget. Eventually I had a recital. It was in Englewood Elementary School. Teachers, parents, students, and Mrs. Cox were there. Of course, one gets nervous butterflies, etc. My recital went perfectly from start to finish. I got a lot of compliments. Kai had recitals way past me. She continues to have the piano we practiced on. As for me, I play the bongos and some acoustic guitar.

Pets

Family with Poki and Malu when I was in college.

Back in Coos Bay, when I lived at home our family had two pets. One was a big gray Himalayan cat we called Malu, Hawaiian for the "Quiet one". After he was neutered, and lost his wild side, he was still awful tough. He kept the vermin away from the house. He also had ferocious cat fights with the other cats. We could hear it at night. He came home after one evenings scrap; with a claw stuck in the top of his head. He had grooves on his head through the many fights he had.

Malu loved us, and we loved him. He would look at you. Pounce on you and make himself comfortable on you as you were watching the T.V. He didn't play favorites. But he was dad's cat. One day Malu was crying and dad saw Malu on the fence with a large trap caught on his stomach skin flap. Malu had yanked out the stake and chain, and somehow got home. Dad immediately took Malu to the Vet where the trap was removed, and Malu got stitched up. Dad tried in vain to find out who had set that trap. No one would admit it if they did. After 19 years Malu got terminal cancer. The doctor giving him a lethal injection. He died at home in Dad's arms. His eyes closed and he was gone.

Our other pet was a small Shelty. Dad named him Poki, Hawaiian for the Boss. Everybody in the neighborhood knew Poki. Everyone who met Poki liked him. He had quite the reputation. He too was tough, but in a different sense. Poki was strictly an outside dog. Mom would not allow him in the house. Poki had his own dog house; he also had the front porch, or yard to roam. Poki ran away from home a couple of times. Once we had to retrieve him from the dog pound. The other time he was gone for a while. We thought we might have lost him for good. He did find his way home. A complete stinky mess.

Poki loved the outdoors. When we went mushroom picking, he would herd us, as it was bred in him. He always looked like he had a smile out there. Poki was a superb swimmer. You could hold on to his tail. He would tow you to the other side of the lake if need be. As Poki aged he developed arthritis. He had bad glaucoma in his eyes. You could see that he was just suffering. I think he was about 14, or 15 years old when he passed, which is a long life for such high-strung dogs. One day I was going to the Hall to try for a job. I reversed my truck. I knew immediately that it was Poki under the rear right tire. I pulled forward, got out, and saw Poki. I shouted out "Oh Shit" in despair. Dad came running out of the house and he fell down by Poki. Dad told me to go to the Hall. I did! When I came home. Dad told me he put a gun to Poki's head and put him out of misery. He was buried immediately by Dad, next to Malu. Those two will always be remembered by us. They were such an integral part of our lives, and they will be remembered.

Guns

At an early age I was introduced to guns, primarily BB and an antique single shot pump pellet gun, with a power equivalency of a 22-caliber rifle, if pumped five or more times. All were open sites, no scopes. I would target practice with dad, learning his breathing and squeezing of the trigger technique.

I had a couple of friends when I was in 7th grade, David Kiander and Arnie Crane. We would go to the forested areas near their houses and shoot at targets, vermin, etc. There was a light moon out one early day. David fired a shot up in the air. He said I just shot the moon. How do you know? He replied, "I could hear the ricochet." We all laughed.

One year, when it was Black-tailed deer season, my schoolmate Chet and I were going hunting on Weyerhaeuser land. The day before we did some target shooting to home in our sights. The next day we were off, hoping to land that elusive buck. Chet and I split up from the get-go. After about two hours of tromping around it was beginning to look bleak. I was at the bottom of a ravine when up above there was rustling in the trees and brush. I fired a shot up that way and ran up the hill. When I got through all the brush and trees there was a large clear-cut area. Standing and looking at me was a herd of Elk. They looked at me as if I were some sort of dummy. I fired two shots in the air. They slowly moved out, still watching.

When I was fishing out of Kodiak, when on the marshy shore we would have guns for bears. I carried an AK 47. Never had to use it. For the helluvit, I fired off a powerful handgun, not using proper technique and only one hand. When I fired, I wasn't properly positioned. I thought I tore my arm off at the shoulder. The backlash practically knocked me on my ass. That was a learning lesson. Know the weapon you are shooting or find out how. I always loved this quip by Charles Bronson: Guns don't scare me. "Idiots" with guns scare me.

Car

I first learned to drive in a 1956 worn out Willy's Jeep. It would never say die. It had a flathead 6-cylinder engine. It was very slow and loud. We had it for years. Its primary use was for hauling firewood. Dad had me splitting wood. Eventually I was using the chain saw. Dad and I went to Bullards Beach in Bandon. We saw a man trying to pull a large root stump out with his winch. He couldn't do it and gave up. Dad, having that great eye, saw a tree with a huge limb. He backed under the limb. Than dad and I attached our long big chain along with a thick rope to the Jeep. We than put a wrap on that root stump. The rope and the chain were over the limb. We slowly tightened the chain until everything was tight. We put the Jeep in 4-wheel, changing the hubs and then yanked it. That root stump jumped in the air, just under the limb and into the bed of the Willy's. It was an amazing calculation by dad. We took all the gear off and crawled home in that loud Willy. That root stump is one center piece of a number of wood masterpieces by dad and a friend. Just Gorgeous. That was a good recreational day for Dad and me.

Back when I had just got my permit to drive dad had gotten a new four-wheel drive- and got rid of the old Willy jeep. Mind you this truck was a Datsun, and jeep conversion wasn't brand new, just to us. I had just got home from some type of practice. Dad and mom were waiting by the driveway. Dad told me to pick up Kane from swim practice and meet the rest of the family at the Langley's for dinner. I went to the Mingus park pool and picked up Kane. I told him we were taking the new Datsun to Indian Legends, a very rugged trail running into the brush at the end of California Street to sorta test the truck. This turned out to be a dumb stunt, because it was raining heavy. Indian Legends was thick mud; and the mountain trajectory was steep. What the hell, huh? I didn't know back then that if you locked in the hubs in the wheels there would be good four-wheel motion. Instead, I gunned it from the bottom of Indian Legends to the very top and onto the other side. Kane bumped his head many times. I thought that I was going to flip the truck or worse, by getting it stuck in the middle of the mountain. We had made it through the Indian legend's treachery to the top of California Street, where we coasted down to the Langley's house. Bobby Langley was waiting outside and couldn't believe his eyes. By the way, Kane and I ate really fast. We excused ourselves and took the truck home. It was a total muddy mess. Kane and I washed it off as fast as possible. When mom and dad got home the only question, they had for us was, "Why is the driveway so wet?" Well, how could we know that? That's it!

Vacations

Oregon is such a beautiful State. We went to places all over Oregon and it was almost always fun. As youngsters with mom and dad, we explored the Oregon caves, a wonderful, natural beauty. We went to Crater Lake, an awesome huge crater, with a great scenic view. Diamond Lake in the winter was nothing but deep white snow. We spotted a silver fox, with tints of blue, truly a spectacular sight. We went to Central Oregon, desert, lava beds etc. Oregon is so diverse with its many different sights and views.

Whenever friends, and family came to visit we made a point of taking them to the Redwoods, just past Brookings Oregon and Crescent City, California. It was always fun walking amongst the great giants.

Jamaica

Our trip to Jamaica was fun from the start. Yah, Mon! We flew out of Portland to Dallas to Miami. The plane trip to Jamaica was cancelled for some reason. All of us, mom, dad, Kai, and her boyfriend, David Yoast. Finally, AFS student Natasha Tangira, and myself. We had to stay the night in humid Miami because the plane was held over. We stayed in a motel close to the airport. The next day we were off to Jamaica. We flew over Cuba into Jamaica to Montego Bay. We were on our way to our Hotel in

Negril. The bus trip to the hotel was wild. Little Jamaican kids trying to sell large bags of Ganja (Marijuana). As a matter of fact, the culture was built on selling something worth nothing for money, sort of like Nogales, or Tijuana. It is based on an economy that has very little to offer except tourism. We got to Negril and I immediately went to my hut and crashed. I must have been the only one who was dead-tired. The next day I was totally refreshed. I saw that dad was eating a Jamaican egg breakfast from a local lady. She wanted $20 so mom forked out an American twenty-dollar bill. Little did we know, there was an exchange for Jamaican money which was much less than our money, a lesson learned right away.

We had a good time in Jamaica. We experienced excellent food and later, many fun adventures. We met a young tall, big Jamaican black man. His name was Ronald. He and a couple friends would cater us at his café and take us on wonderful tours during the day. At night the cantina was open. The pool room was open too, just one pool table with a few pool cues. It just so happened the Jamaican champ was in Negril. I was getting quite hot on that pool table. I hadn't lost a match. The so-called Jamaican champ and I had a one game dual. We were evenly matched, but when it came to the last shot it was mine. I was going to take what was normally considered the last fair shot before someone shouted, "Jamaican Rules." This meant that I had no choice but to make it their way or lose. I put all my concentration and focus on this near impossible shot. I took my cue and chalked it. Then I went to the pool table. I basically guessed how to go about it. It had to be a hard shot. I took my time, then cracked the cue ball. The solid ball I hit went on a miraculous ride from one side to the other side to the right hole. Just like it was being guided by radar in a rough and tumble way. I made that shot and beat Jamaican rules. There were quite a few people. There was a loud applause. I still couldn't believe it. Best Pool game I ever played. I was now the Jamaican champ!

We had a big adventure on a wide river in the tropical forest. All of us who could swim did. We floated down and across the river underneath a huge waterfall. Inside the waterfall was a ledge we walked on to get to a pool of water. It was very cool! We all came out the way we came in, then crossed the river farther down on the other side and walked back up the bank to the starting point. What a thrill that was.

Another neat day of swimming was near or with the crocodiles. Supposedly they are harmless. Just fish eaters we were told. Some had grown up to seventeen feet in length. There was a man who could feed and pet the crocodiles. There were also crocodiles with their mouths wide open trying to burn the leeches from the insides of their mouths. They didn't look real.

We had an interest into going to Kingston, the Capitol. Ronald advised us against it. Apparently, it can be quite dangerous. Our meals were excellent in Jamaica - jerk pork, jerk chicken, beef, and baked fish, all seasoned and good.

Most of us were out in the ocean for a swim when a boat came floating by us and tried to sell us boat rides. I mean, these guys would stop at nothing to make a sale. Another time we were heading up to the Café when a voice called out to us. Mom shouted out, "Why don't you leave us alone already?" That voice was Ronald's. He was smiling because he knew about all the sell jobs that we had to go through.

I will comment on the beauty of Jamaica. Crystal clear blue ocean water, rivers everywhere, beautiful country and scenery. We had spent a week in Jamaica. Then back to the home front for all of us.

Costa Rica

Our family vacation to Costa Rica included my three-year-old nephew Koa. We flew from Portland to Houston and onto Costa Rica. We flew into San Jose, the Capitol. We met with our guides at the airport. One was holding up an Ahuna sign, which was funny because the trip was booked under Yoast. The driver of the van was Mario. The guide was Carlos, a good, interesting, and at times a fun, guy.

We learned the staple food was rice and beans, along with fresh fruit. We went to the volcanos and watched the lava flow. Everything was tropical where we started, much like Hawaii. Those of us brave enough went down a Zip-line. It was the longest zip-line in the world at the time, three miles to be exact. We went from one stop to the next until the end. You could probably go as fast as you wanted; however, you had to control your speed near every stop. The view was breathtaking, over the top of trees, and such.

From the mountains we went to the Beach, a long ride in the van, with several stops for food and sightseeing. The beach was wonderful. We had great accommodations. I went surfing and caught some good waves. Then I suffered from severe sunburn. I forgot to put on the sunscreen and paid the price for it. There was wonderful seafood soups, pizza, and excellent ceviche. Just great. Not far from the beach was the border of Nicaragua, with barbed wire and armed soldiers. In the trees there were monkeys and birds, swinging and fluttering around.

We ended in San Jose where we started. We checked out the city before we flew out of Costa Rica to home. I would highly recommend a Costa Rica trip to anyone.

Hawaii

Hawaii for me is Spencer-Ahuna or Ahuna-Spencer. I have lots of family on both sides on probably every Hawaiian island. This situation leads to a Smith-Jones scenario. No one knows everyone, so one must be cordial as if with a complete stranger.

Hunting

I took my hunter safety course at a very young age. The instructor was Bill Wankin. I passed easily. I put that card to its first test on the big island of Hawaii.

Dad, Kane, and I went to Laupoehoe on the big island of Hawaii to hunt wild pigs. There we met with Uncle Shine and his friend Pach. There were two kids and two hunting dogs which proved to be worthless. We were to climb a high hill. That was a ten-mile hike straight up a narrow gravel road. Uncle Shine and Pach carried the rifles. They were 30.30 caliber weapons. We carried the other stuff - food, bags, etc.

Uncle Shine set the pace, and never slowed down. Pach was way behind, and he yelled, "Shine, the dogs gotta take a shit!" We all laughed to ourselves as Uncle Shine just increased his pace. When we made it to the ten-mile marker I was with Uncle Shine. I don't know or remember where the rest of the party went. Those stupid dogs kept chasing and sometimes killing the baby pigs (keiki). They were really of no use to us.

Uncle Shine and I found a meadow amongst the tropical forest. Standing in the middle of the meadow was a big boar. His profile was facing us. He didn't know or sense that we were there. Uncle Shine quickly raised his rifle, took aim, and fired. It was a head shot, the boar fell, quivered and died. Uncle Shine went right to work, first skinning the pig in which the guts fell. But before he quartered the pig, he cut out the lower jaw bone for me. Traditionally a large abalone shell is wired in place when the jaw bone is solid white; and the tusks and mandible are in a down position. You can put candy or a little sand in the open shell for an ashtray. Then Uncle Shine quartered the pig and put it in canvas bags. I carried my share.

Klaus, Kai, Grandma Edna, Kane with dad and mom in the background.

That pig had to have been 180 pounds quartered out. We carried the pig and the rifle out to the main trail.

We met up with everyone else on the main trail. The dogs were still chasing the baby pigs. Pach nailed a big Boar, all dressed and bagged. The hunting trip didn't get any easier since we had to pack those bags and rifles ten miles downhill. Uncle Shine told me when he shot that pig there was even a bigger one nearby. I didn't see it.

All I can say about that hunting trip was that it was an experience of a lifetime - something I will never forget. We went a couple other times, but the experience was just not the same.

Hawaii dive

You always hear of those high cliff divers diving into shallow waters, primarily in Mexico. There is just such a place on the big island of Hawaii. Hilo to be exact, just behind the high school nestled in palm trees and lush tropical growth. The water below is a deep ice pond. The cliffs range from 80 ft. to 20 ft. high. There are some areas too dangerous to jump from. My uncles Jay and Kihei showed us this wonder, along with cousin Dukie. Back then I did jump from the highest spot more than a few times. You had to jump out so as not to bounce off the rocks. This area was called "South America".

When we were on the Big Island, of Hawaii during the summer of 1988, we spent some time in a small fishing village named Millolii, a quaint small place by the ocean. Uncle Skinny Tahara had access to a building to clean fish, cook etc. So nice! The guys decided to go skin diving, and pick Ophe (Limpets).

While the women, mom and Nona, Skinny's wife, stayed ashore, I was out snorkeling on top of the water with a spear floating about and pushing myself with my fins. I got to water that was 15' to 20' deep. I saw some movement below. I saw the antennae knowing it was a lobster and a big one at that. It saw me and was reaching for me. I obliged him and dived down and speared him in his chest plate, bringing him up to the surface. I took the lobster to the building. Funny, nobody was there! I put it on a picnic table on the inside of the building. Then back to the ocean to see if there were more lobsters. I ran into Kane, and an East German refugee named Burt. Burt was invited by dad to go to Hawaii with us. He turned out to be a

real schmuck. Kane was the one who found my lobster. It had made its way off the table and around a corner of a wall. It was sensing its way back to the ocean. We all had some of that lobster. Skinny ate the meat in the head with glee. As it turned out, I could have had a big fine. Lucky the evidence was in our stomachs.

Ahuna Reunion

We flew into Honolulu International Airport for our families first Hawaiian Christmas. We stayed a couple days and nights at the Queen Kapulani hotel with a spectacular view of Diamond Head. It is near the Zoo. The Queen's bath is right by us. There was a big Christmas tree in the lobby. We went to visit Uncle Shine and Aunty Cheiko. It was good to see Uncle. Aunty wasn't feeling well at the time. The next day I went out on the balcony of our room. Seeing a TV crew and recognizing some actors even from the 7th floor. They were setting up for Hawaii five O. I let my wife know that they were going to film Five O below. She said, "I want to meet Danno." So, we went down, to possibly hob-knob with celebrities. We went down and wanted to take pictures. A big Hawaiian woman waved her hand, she said, "No! No!" So, we stayed a short while and then left. From

Family visits Uncle Shine. From left mom, Kane, Dad and myself.

Oahu we flew to the Big Island of Hawaii. We stayed most of a week at Uncle Billy's motel, right by the ocean. There was an Ahuna Reunion at the beach in Keaukaha with traditional Hawaiian food and Hawaiian music led by dad, surrounded by his cousins. We ate our fill and talked amongst ourselves. Uncle Robert Shioji wasn't doing so well. He could eat like a horse; yet so sickly skinny. He passed away shortly after we left the islands, later in the week. We took in Aunty Aloha's Ceremony of life. She was my grandmother's sister, a very special lady. It was held in a big Pavilion. I saw uncles, aunties, cousins, and friends that I hadn't seen in years. There must have been close to 200 people there. Later, in the water, Dad, Kane, and I swam with a small sea turtle. When we flew out from the islands most of the memories were good.

South America

When our family went back to Hawaii after our college graduations, I took Kai, and Kane to South America. Kai hated me at first because she got attacked by vicious mosquitos. I had forgot that she was so susceptible to them. As soon as we reached the ice pond, and she got in the bugs went away. Kane and I went to the top. He jumped in. I discovered that I didn't have the "no fear factor" anymore so I went to a lower level and jumped in. It felt good that I had shown my sister and brother something that most people never see.

Hapuna Beach

One year, dad and I were at Hapuna beach in Hawaii swimming, talking, and watching the pretty girls go by. It was really relaxing. We were heading out to shower when I heard, "Hey Klaus." I looked, and it was a friend, Marty Gardener, a fellow longshoreman from Portland. Marty was in a car with his dad, mom, and wife. They had just come down from the volcano. Sometimes life can be funny that way.

Sports

I was happy to graduate from High School

High school was sports and studies in that order. When all was said and done, I had accomplished some things: four-year letterman in wrestling, District 5AAA Champ, Boys State representative, Good Citizen, most inspirational wrestler. All this gave me a potentially good scholarship to Linfield, in McMinnville. Coach Bob Walker, a big guy, wanted me to be his Wrestling Captain. He also happened to be one of the football coaches on a national caliber team. I probably could have been a part of that team too. I turned it all down to stay at home and go to Junior college.

Baseball

A long time ago I played baseball. Some might say, "Wait a minute. How can you remember that far back?" Some might say, "It's an elephant's reserve bank memory." Others might say, "Great recall mechanisms." I just say, "It was good friends, good coaches, and a helluva lot of fun as kids." I don't know. I played for two teams as a youngster. We took a close second to the Eagles T-ball when I was with the Crows. We each got Dairy Queen ice cream for the effort.

The next season I played hardball fast pitch for the Yankee's. I played shortstop. I don't remember that much about that season. We must have been good though, after all we were the Yankee's!! They are still my favorite team. I never continued with baseball. Instead I switched to track and field. I really excelled at that sport as a youngster.

Football

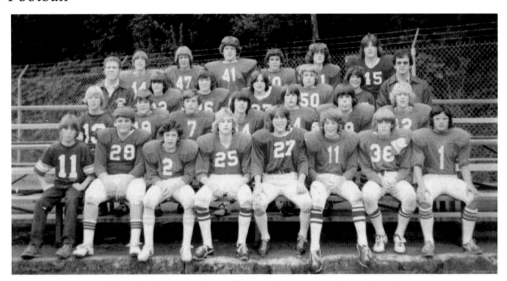

My eighth-grade football team. I am in row 1, number 1.

Football was something every kid wanted to be a part of. Dad let me play, yet he was totally against the sport. In 8th grade football, through the Junior Varsity season. The coaches let me play offense, defense, and special teams. We didn't win much but it was so much fun being or trying to be where the action was. I wanted to sit out my senior season of football at Marshfield. I didn't like the scheme of things; however, Tom Jenkins, my coach, talked me into it by saying that it would be my final year to play football and it would put me in great shape for wrestling. Both statements were false. We had a bad team with a lot of potential. Also, I was in the worst shape of my life for a wrestling start. My senior season of football SUCKED!!

The best shot I had of playing football in college was at Linfield in McMinnville, OR. They have a national caliber team practically every year. I turned wrestling and everything else down to go to Junior college. After two years at JC, I took a year off to work. Then I went back to school in Eugene. I wanted to be a student athlete there. I ended up being a wrestler. I wanted to play football but when I walked by Rich Brooks' office, I saw just how big those guys were. I doubt I would have made the team.

The Wrestler

I started wrestling in 4th grade. I went undefeated and liked winning a lot. When I got to high school the local radio station would announce my victories. Winning was always it, or why do it. I lost my share too. I was voted Team Co- Captain along with Mark Bessey, an exceptional athlete during my senior year at Marshfield. I ended with a 25-win season with three losses. The District Championships was really the end of the season. Not that we didn't compete at state. We had one placer, our 98 pounder (Conrad Eisle). Coach Lynn Mathews was quite a motivational coach. Coach Tom Jenkins was a good wrestler in his time. Finally, the assistant coach, Wayne Van Burger, was always there for you -a good man.

1976

1976 is a year I will always remember. My grades were good, all A's and one B. I excelled at everything that year. On the track I was unbeatable in the 1320 meter, three laps around the track, setting a school record which was broke the following year by Ken Loftus during Ken's year, 1977, my last year of Marshfield Jr. High, my 8th grade year. Back to 1976, there was a State meet in Springfield for those who qualified. I ran the mile and led the pack for almost the whole race. I came in 4th place with a time of 5:25.5 exactly, not bad for a 7th grader. If there were archives back, then that record would still be there. I developed a nickname. Most everybody still called me Klaus, but many in my class started calling me "Gator". Some still do! I don't know if it was from those Gator McKlusky action movies starring Burt Reynolds, or what. It just seemed to stick through junior high. It was good while it lasted.

On a different note, the Portland Trailblazers won the NBA World Championship. What a year!

5AAA Wrestling

During 1981, going toward spring, it was the District 5AAA wrestling tournament held at North Eugene High School. This being to qualify for the State tournament held at David Douglas High School in Portland. I was the number one seed in my weight class. I proceeded to go through my first two opponents easy enough. The next day would be the semi-finals. It would be a toughie during the semi-final. I was going against a cross town rival from North Bend. The match went the whole three rounds. It ended in a tie.

It now was overtime. I was tired, and I knew that he was exhausted. I won 7 to 4 in overtime. Mom said she was on pins and needles throughout the match. Kai was "Miss Confident" that I would win. That was a big win for me. It boosted my confidence for the finals, which I won handily.

Tough guy competition

I am a sports fan, so anything that revolves around sports; is something I would like. I fought in a Tough Guy competition during the last part of my senior year. I really had no choice but to do it. My name had been put on a card to fight another guy from the opposing town in the local newspaper - The World. I found out later that the heavyweights, usually the main draw, didn't even show for the fight.

The guy I fought had a 20 lb. advantage. We had wrestled against each other before. I had won. As the fight started. I walked into a big left hand. Later dad said, "Did you even feel it!" Apparently not, because for the rest of the round we were winging punches at each other. His punch woke me up. I know that I had control of the fight after that round, throwing straight left jabs, and strong right crosses. At the end of the fight there was the decision. The winner is KLAUS-silence. Then the other guy was awarded the decision. The other guy's coach, Dave Abraham, told me, "But you had fun Klaus. It was fun." That pissed me off and Abe knew it as he backed away. I will say this about Abe. I was one of just a few wrestlers allowed to wrestle with his guys from North Bend. He even gave me a ride home from freestyle Greco State Competition, in Salem. For that I was grateful. The next day after the fight I got a call from a teammate's dad, saying I had won. Some other people who had seen it said the same thing. Just knowing that much made the outcome not so bad.

Wrestling – Jr. College

During high school, I had opportunities and options to one really nice expensive college - Linfield in McMinnville. I don't know why I didn't go that route. Instead, I decided to stay home and go to Southwestern Oregon Community College. I took Basic Studies and was

Southwestern Oregon Community College was the setting for a regional wrestling tournament last weekend, during which SWOCC grappler Klaus Ahuna ... 134-pound weight class. Ahuna won honors as "most outstanding wrestler" at the meet, and will go on to national championships.

(Photo by Bruce Smith)

on the wrestling and track teams. John Speasl was the wrestling and women's volleyball coach. We went to a Dave Schultz seminar in Southern Oregon State College. It was all about headlocks, and choke-outs. Dave and his brother Mark were Olympic champions. The book the Foxcatcher, tells the life story of these brothers and the tragic taking of Dave's life. The movie is good too.

The biggest wrestling match that I can account for was in the Region 18 Championships. This was held in my home town of Coos Bay at the Prosper Hall on the South West Oregon Community College campus (SWOCC). I was to wrestle George Patterson, from Northern Idaho, in the finals. George was a third-place finisher at the National Tournament the previous year. I came out blazing with a takedown, reversal, and an escape. In the third period, George caught me with an over/under throw. I lost by fall. I qualified 2nd for the Junior College National Tournament. The tournament was held in Worthington, Minnesota. At the tournament, I quite simply stunk. I fell way behind, fought back valiantly, but fell one point short. This eliminated me from the tournament. George cheered me on throughout the match. He ended up being the 134-pound National Champion. My High School District Championship, and my brief stint on the travel squad at the University of Oregon did not compare to that one night in my hometown.

Wrestling mentor

My wrestling mentor, Sergio Gonzales, was a small Mexican man. Sergio was a World class Olympic wrestler in his time. He used altitude training in his Jacksonville, Oregon environment. Though I was bigger than Sergio, I could never escape from him. I trained for close to a week before I had to fly off to Nationals in Minnesota. Sergio knew me as a high school sophomore. He saw potential in me, as did other coaches. Dad always stuck with the best. That is why he took me to be trained by Sergio. Sergio was the best.

Surfing

Here are some basics of surfing for those who want to go in deeper water, where the good waves are. First, you better know how to swim. Second, you should be in good shape. Believe me,

Surfing on the Oregon coast.

Surfing at Coos Bay the day I personally experienced hyperventilation.

paddling out through the small stuff takes it out of you. Wearing a good light wetsuit helps in cold water. Third, buddy up, especially in isolated areas. If you surf in warm water - California, Florida, Hawaii, or a number of other places in this world - prepare for territorial rights in the water. In other words, some surfers claim areas as their own. Make sure your wetsuit is a good fit. A tight fit could lead to hyperventilation, not a good thing in the water.

For those of you who don't know much about surfing, it has evolved into an acrobatic show, with guys on small twin fins cutting up the waves. Then there are those fearless guys who take on the gigantic waves, a force of nature. They are practically tidal waves about four miles from the beach in Maui and spots in California. I'm sure there are other areas around the world like that. Some guys fly out by chopper. Their safety net is a jet ski to round them up or find them if they should fall. Dangerous, exciting, and dramatic. The key would be not to fall, nothing but powerful thick fast-moving ocean water. Even a power cord has its stretchability limits. If you're under, you must hope the jet ski is nearby or you are probably done for.

Now that I've told you all these horrible things, have fun! Really, start up in the small stuff. Let the waves carry you on your board. Have a seasoned surfer beside you in waist deep water. The surfer will point you in the right direction to the shore. He will tell you to paddle hard. Once the wave picks up your board, and you are moving, put your hands on the rails (the sides of the board). Get to your knees, then work your way to a standing position. Guess What? You're surfing now. That's the real fun of it.

In the summer of 1979, I bought a used surfboard - a swallowtail, in Honolulu. It was 6' 3", beat-up but rideable. I brought it home to Coos Bay where dad put a leash on it. My sophomore year in high school I surfed with two brothers from California. I do believe that we were the first to surf the southwest Oregon coast. There never was anyone out there but seals and seabirds. We went out during small craft warnings. My senior year there was the Outlook Magazine story had an issue with me on the cover. It was written by Travis Johnson, a classmate. It turned out good!

Puhiki

I will not make a big hubbub about Puhiki on the big island of Hawaii, but it was a scary moment. Dad and I entered the water and we kicked our way out to the good surf. I caught a nice wave and rode it almost all the way in. As I kicked out to return for more, I noticed dad had gone to a dangerous area of coral reef, where big waves were crashing, and then leaving only a few inches of water over the coral. I made a bee-line to him and found that he had lost one of his fins and had been carried there by the current. Suddenly a ten-foot wave was upon us and I dove through the wave leaving him to fend for himself. After the wave went past, I went back and found him there with a puncture wound on the bottom of his foot. He said he still knew how to roll like the limo elle elli (seaweed). I knew we had to get off the reef so when there was a small break in the waves, I had dad put an arm over my shoulder and we managed to limp off the reef and get to shore. As we were about to leave, a young boy came by and gave dad his missing fin. I made a comic book called "The Wave." Those fortunate enough have a copy and know the story. I think I can make more, but for sale only!

Honolii

Dad and I were in Hawaii on the Big Island a while back. Anyway, there is a surfers' beach called Honolii. The waves are way down a cliff that you can walk down with your equipment. We had Boogie boards and fins. The water is always dirty because the trucks from up above knock down dirt and debris into the water. The ocean is also an estuary, where fresh water mixes with the salt water, making for dangerous undertows. Well, dad and I were having fun with the waves when somehow, I drifted into that estuary. I got sucked under for what seemed like five minutes. I didn't panic, and it spit me up. I wasn't ready to do any more surfing that day. I was shaken up. I watched dad catch a nice wave in. When dad came riding in on the next wave, he had that happy smile. Dad asked, "Did you get sucked under?" I told him, "Yes." He said, "Same with me." We really should have known better. We left. The very next day we heard about a fatality at Honolii. The surfer got sucked in, panicked and drowned. Apparently, he was some hot-shot Coast Guard rescue guy. Dad's eyes got big. I'm sure I had that same look.

Smashed by Sandy Beach

The ocean is such a powerful entity. It was summer and I was just about to start high school. Our family flew into Oahu. An hour later dad's cousin Mome took us to the famous bodysurfing beach Sandy Beach. I was the first one out in the surf. I was bobbing around, when the water fell to my knees. I knew I was doomed. I was too far in front of the wave to dive through it. The only chance I had was to go for it and hope for the best. The wave picked me up, smashed me in the sand with all its force. When the water receded, I was a crumpled, but not broken, body. I could barely stand, and I was all hunched over in pain. Mome came running in the sand. But the worst wasn't over for me. Dad gave me a good berating, telling me, "You always relax and roll with the wave." He was pissed off. I was just over the hurt the wave did. I chipped a tooth and was coated with sand all over. Lucky enough, I was resilient enough to bounce back. Sandy Beach was all it was made out to be, and more.

Young Man Working Through Life

When employed with the Coos Forest Patrol, my 1st paying job. Larry Mollers was my boss, a helluva good guy. I got that through my good friend Jim Mollers, his son. With the Coos Forest Patrol, we did slash burns, fought dunes fires, and did a lot of maintenance on the Forest Patrol vehicles and equipment. That was a good job. My brother and sister went to Europe that summer and I said, "No, I want to work on the Forest Patrol and make some money."

Crab

Crab is a seafood delight, especially right out of the steam kettle. One day years ago when I was in sixth or seventh grade, dad took us crabbing in our eleven-foot aluminum boat. We were all strapped up with Life vests. We put in by the North Bend airport. We could keep twelve legal males each. When we left, we had just that much - forty-eight keepers and some were real big ones. We took them home and steamed them up in their own saltwater. Than we let them cool. Dad was right on it." Does everybody want Crab Louie?" "Yes," we said. If I remember correctly, mom was in Germany, so dad became the crab chef cook. Crab cocktail, grilled crab sandwiches, crab omelets. Man, I'm just saying that we got crabbed out with Dad. Anyway, it made for a wonderful story until we could eat no more.

Dad gave me the boat and trailer. Kane and I, and sometimes a friend; would put in at the North Bend ramp near the Airport. We would have our Crab traps, bait and maybe a lunch. At the dock we would row out to the nearest buoy, tie off bait in our pots and toss them in and wait. The sunny days were really relaxing. You could get up to 36 crab per person back then and you didn't need a shellfish license. Life was Bliss. We

Kane with largest crab of the day!

normally got our limit of Dungeness, plus we kept the big red rock crab. Their meat is sweeter. Those were the days. They are gone now. Just memories.

Another time I took Kane and one of his school chums, Tom Ward crabbing on a beautiful flat ocean day. I had gone out earlier by myself. We loaded up with crab - thirty-six of them. We got a good tan to boot. Good fun!

Alaska

In the summer of 1983, I had my first real experience on a Marine Fishing Vessel was in Kodiak, Alaska on the fishing vessel, Silver Fox - a 32-foot Salmon Seiner. The owner and skipper were Jerry Byler. He had two sons, Darrin and Eric, who worked on boats also owned by Jerry. Jerry believed in character, and he was a fair and good man. I ended up being a deckhand/lead man thanks to my friend Greg Go-Go Guerra, also a wrestler. There was another guy, Willie Weaver, and later an Arkansas boy named Brock Overton. Brock, Willie, and I worked in a fish cannery before the season really started. Jerry let us stay on the boat.

Three months of fishing for salmon turned out lousy due to El Nino. After the season Jerry knew he had to get us home. He paid us adequately enough to get home. I decided to stay so I could get on a King Crabber. No luck so I worked in a grocery store. That didn't last long so I flew back home to Coos Bay.

The next spring, I went to Seattle to work on a 210-foot processor. The skipper was a big Hawaiian named Bill Kukahiko, or Ipo. He was family to my dad. We ended up crossing the Bering Sea. We processed herring out of Togiak. Later we traveled to almost the top of the world, first to a small village called Platinum and then on past the Norton Sound. You could see how Christopher Columbus estimated that the earth was round. You could see that from up there. On the processor there was a lot of liquor and pot. I got caught up in a lot of that. Somehow, I made it back to Coos Bay a pitiful rundown wreck. That was the last of my Alaskan adventures. I could go back sometime in the future.

College

The University of Oregon (UofO) was a huge school. I opted for Secondary Education and Coaching. To tell you the truth, it always seemed like I was running on ball bearings there. I found out that I was sinking backwards with bad grades while practicing and competing with the wrestling team at the same time.

The University of Oregon was sort of cool. I mean, there were World class athletes all around. I saw Mary Slaney running around Hayward track as I was doing stair laps. Her husband, a discus thrower, was on his bike, I guess trying to keep up with her. He was a giant. Joaquim Cruz, the Olympic 800-meter champion, was in my speech class, not to mention the number of football and basketball players vying to make their next step to the pros. The school was a mecca for big time athletes. Like I said, sort of cool being a Duck.

Elizabeth Bressan was the only PhD that was positive toward me in the program as well as Mike Reuter in the Professional Activities wrestling course. I quit Secondary Education, in order to try and dig myself out of a big hole. Believe it or not I did. I landed my Bachelor of Science degree by switching to the Aqua program headed by Don van Rossen and the Leisure program which often had the same classes. I finally got some form of physiology down. I didn't go to the commencement with my spectacular 2.21 average in an accredited program. As I was to say later, all I wanted to do was wipe my ass with that degree. I couldn't land a job right out of school with that degree. Now I think the degree is good for communication.

My first summer at U of O. I was arrested and taken to jail. I got in an altercation with two cops. I was on one pedal of my bike kicking off to get to class faster. The incident happened in the downtown Mall. I wasn't wearing a shirt, just my backpack, shorts, and slippers. The cop stepped in front of me and stopped me. I lurched forward and stopped. Right off he was a real prick, asking for my license, which I gave him. It was a hot day, and I tried to explain to him that I had a class to go to. I reached a hand out for my license but he thought I was attacking him. He then proceeded to start hitting me with his lead billy club. He had a buddy that was whacking me from behind. Eventually I gave up and let them handcuff me. They hauled me off to jail. While I was in jail getting booked, there was this fine blonde cop inside. She smiled at me and said, "You work-out." You have a nice build." I was damn near naked for Chrissake's. I was in the peak of my conditioning. She served me a plate of some good grub and gave me a bag of cigarette tobacco. I was sleeping when my sister came and bailed me out.

I then had to find a lawyer, which put me right in front of my parents. Some longshoreman had told dad that a lawyer out of Cottage Grove. Francis Linklater was good. Dad paid him a large sum of money to defend me and get both charges, assault and resisting arrest, dropped. As it turned out, he had no intention of defending me at all. So, I told dad that I was gonna get my own lawyer. I did. A member of the student body government recommended Ken Morrow. He said he believed my story. He would take it to court. This whole fiasco turned out to be very expensive for mom and dad, especially since we dropped that large sum on Linklater. Now they had to pick-up court charges for Morrow. On court day I had three excellent witnesses go to the stand for me: Ray Prefontaine, Ron Finley, my wrestling coach, and George Wasson, a counselor. These men got the assault charge dropped.

However, I don't believe that Ken Morrow wanted to give me a clean slate by having all the charges dropped. I was right. Ken made sure the resisting arrest charge stuck. That gave me 500 hours of community service. Ken actually was kind enough to set me up with Eugene Sports Program (ESP) as a coach for the sixth-grade flag football team. As the season progressed, we improved but I don't think we won a game. The kids were good kids, but we couldn't get past my inexperience as a coach. After that my community service was done.

I was supposed to have the resisting arrest charge expunged. Well, I found out some years later when I applied for a valet job at the Mill Casino. That charge was still on my record. The Tribal Council was cool, however and thought the charge was all in college fun. They hired me anyway.

Charyl (Martie) Reid

Martie and I met in Bend, Oregon. I was commuting back and forth from Black Butte Ranch at Sisters. I had a Quad in the summer of 1986. Martie had a room just below me. I would go to the Ranch to lifeguard and teach swim lessons. Sometimes I would stay at the ranch and party. Other times I would spend time with Martie. Martie was separated with two kids, a girl named Melanie and a boy named Micah. Both would visit her occasionally. Martie was still married to a small man. His name was Marty as well. The kids were theirs. Throughout the summer, Martie and I got really close. We spent nights together often. She was seven years older than me. She was quite a lady. When the summer was almost over, I had to go back to school to finish one more term. Martie asked if she could go with me. I said, "Sure." We would live together. When we got to Eugene. I was back in school. Martie had to scrape by yet she got a good job as an accountant. Martie and I had some good times together going to movies, nice dinners, a UofO football game. Life was good. I got a graveyard mill job doing conveyor line work. It lasted two months before the mill let me go (Fired me.). Dad was pissed because he didn't think that I wanted to work because I lost that damn job at the mill. He was partly right. I just couldn't find a job. During this period of time I knocked up Martie. She had an abortion. I suppose we could have worked things out having the baby. We didn't. I had an Internship to complete down in Arizona. I sent materials that was an assignment to Martie. She then forwarded them to my program.

Martie did fly down and visit me. I think that she would have stayed if I had asked her too. I didn't so she flew home. Charyl (Martie) Reid, a good, fine lady!

When I went to the University of Oregon there was a horrific incident that ended up making world news. I had my morning workouts in the Autzen stadium weight room. I had to run there from my dormitory (Carson), then run back after the workout. Later that morning one of the younger wrestlers asked me if I had heard the news. I said, "No, I hadn't." It turns out one of the wrestlers got shot by a sniper. The sniper then shot an Olympic class runner on the outer trail and turned the gun on himself. The sniper was a fraternity student. The runner on the trail died too. That was a very sad day.

My friend, Carolyn Matthews, and I wrote an article together to the Register Guard in Eugene. It was a strong article mentioning how OSU won back-to-back titles (now three Championships). Yes, the state was proud of their accomplishments in baseball. However, Oregon with a big sports base, didn't even have a team. We argued that indeed Oregon should have a team and why. Carolyn did the prep and touch-up work on the article. I signed off on it, K. G. Ahuna, and mailed it off. Oregon indeed has a baseball team now.

It wasn't until we were in our early twenties did my brother and myself finally begin to learn what a Longshoreman was and does. We had just gotten our casual cards from the unemployment office. Before that time Dad had been a Longshoreman for years. We just heard the word Longshoreman. Yah! That's what my dad does. I have been a longshoreman for some thirty years

> Shore side criers "men along the shore" gave rise to the term Longshoreman.

Looking for a way to make a living

Long-haul Trucking

There was a time when I went into Long-Haul truck driving. The South Coast Business Association allowed us guys to take free classes through IITR Truck School. But Dave, the owner of IITR, would not allow me to take the driving test at the Coos Bay Department of Motor Vehicles (DMV). All that studying and driving to be denied a Commercial Driver License (CDL). I found out through a trucking buddy where and when I could be tested in Portland, so I did go for it up there. Where I paid my $250-dollar fee. Drove the course and passed the test. Getting a CDL made me happy at that moment. I found out later how easy it was to lose one.

Now it was on to Oklahoma City. There was an outfit down there called Donco Trading Co. They had Reefer Units (Freezer Containers). A person had to pass two tests in order to work for Donco. The new truckers came from all over. We all stayed at the Radisson Mote). When I went to Oklahoma City, it was 1995 at the time of the bombing by Timothy McVeigh and Terry Nichols. There was FBI, CIA, and any other form of law enforcement running around there. A real melee, total confusion.

As it turned out, I intentionally failed my Donco test simply because, deep down inside, I knew that I didn't want to be a long-haul truck driver. The guy that hired me said, "Now, I gotta get you home." Well the guy gave me a bus ticket home. The trip was OK from Oklahoma to Flagstaff, Arizona. The rest of the trip to Coos Bay was a horror story. I rode into Flagstaff on the Bus. About 1 o'clock in the morning, the continuance was to Los Angeles. I didn't make it out of the Flagstaff bus station until thirteen days later. I somehow either misplaced my bus ticket or lost it. I was doing some crazy things, like hitchhiking to Los Angeles to keep up with my bags. Some bright lights went on right in front of me about 20 miles outside of Flagstaff. It was a Native policeman. He didn't say a word. Just put cuffs on and hauled me off to jail. As soon as I got there, they put me in a cell with a couple other guys. They left me in my street clothes. About every half hour they would take me to a new area. What I saw in that jail, looked like the Holocaust with men just skin and bone living in their own excrement. It was horrible.

After seeing all that, I was put in solitary confinement. I was not allowed a phone call right away. The cell itself had a mat to lay on. I later discovered a toilet. All I wanted was a way home. The time just dragged. All I did was sleep. There was a thick Plexiglas window so you could observe in silence what was going on. The food was no better than pig slop. One day through the window, I saw a chain gang getting ready to go. They were mostly big, tall, long-haired Indians. I kept wondering just how long I was going to stay in that cell. Eventually the food slot would open. Some lady would try to give me pills. I never did take them. But when I was forced to, I would just put them in my mouth and then spit them out later on. I was getting tired of the crap they called food. The guard who served the meals was a big guy who looked like Colonel Sanders. The food would come through a slot. I finally got fed up with it and shoved the tray back in his face. He cleaned up the mess. But I gotta tell you, the food never got any better.

Getting out of there seemed to take an eternity. It ended up being fast. I was taken to the courtroom assisted by a doctor, and a lawyer. When the judge asked whoever, "What is this man in here for?" nobody answered. He practically yelled, "Let him go." It was over. I was out of there after thirteen days. I had estimated sixteen days in my head. Someone had a bus ticket to Coos Bay waiting for me. When I got home, Mom and my baggage were waiting for me.

Longshoring becomes a way of life

At one time in the late 60's and early 70's Coos Bay was the largest port in the world for log exports. Industry flourished - logging, fishing, and log export. I knew that I wasn't going to hang in Coos Bay forever. I was a casual in the area for 15 years. The west coast longshore mix goes from Hawaii to Alaska. Harry Bridges was the main man that was responsible for everything. He had a fantastic eye for the future. His

history continues to lead us today. The man was the leader of the ILWU for years. My father actually had a conversation with Harry. Jack Hall, a Union leader for the workers of Hawaii, came to Coos Bay and stayed with us. Apparently, he had a fond heart for the Hawaiian people.

Longshoremen use pike poles to get logs in place for loading in Coos Bay.

Kane, and I started our venture into Longshoring, getting jobs whenever we could as casuals with white cards, C-status Longshoremen. That began in North Bend/Coos Bay, Oregon. Logs, lumber, paper rolls, and wood chips were the products exported at the time. My dad once said a casual is a man without a country (a casualty). Maybe that is why he always helped the casuals to get registered. As a casual you have to be at the hiring hall, either early morning or early evening. Sometimes you're right on the bubble to be hired when travelers come down and cover the work. That can happen a lot. It really is feast or famine for all working Longshoremen. A lot of the guys I worked with or knew, in Coos Bay are either retired, or dead. Life goes on. Kane left Coos Bay before me, eventually making it to Portland. He really had to put in his time, to solidify his position. I took the long hard road up north to Portland. I put my time in as well.

Longshoring wasn't enough

I don't remember the day. The year was 1988. I had just recently got my white card, casual identification for Longshoring. Kai was already out of the house. Kane was getting ready to leave for Laguna Beach. Me, I didn't know what in the hell I was going to do. Mom made that decision quite simple. "When Kane's gone, you're next to leave." I'm leaving a lot of crap out of this because, frankly, I don't think it's worth writing about. I went to my savings. I took out most of it, traded in my junker Datsun B210 for a better, newer Toyota Tercel Hatchback which ended up being a lifesaver for me.

I lived in that car in Portland for almost two weeks with all my belongings. I finally found a room in the University Apartments, on Lombard Avenue, across the street from a Head Shop. I found a job soon enough. It was as a pizza delivery driver for Pizza Hut. That job lasted about three months. I was fired when I finally told the manager that I wasn't going to deliver cold pizzas anymore.

I finally realized that I had a college degree which wasn't being put to use. I got the Oregonian newspaper and proceeded to send out streams of letters and resumes. I continued to do this with no luck whatsoever. Maybe it was because of my location. St. Johns was sort of a rough area in spots. There was a short stint at Kentucky Fried Chicken as a cook. Finally, I worked at McDonalds so I could get meals. That particular winter was extremely cold, with a wind chill of twenty below zero at times. I was in it walking much of the time.

When I was still in those University apartments, before I became homeless, I was waiting for an Income tax check, some $200. I decided it was time for me to read my Holy Bible. I did from front to back. It didn't make me feel any holier. It did keep me out of trouble. There were a gazillion names that didn't register. The son of the son, etc. The daughter of so and so. I don't remember the book; but the Byrds wrote a song from scripture, Turn! Turn! Turn! That is still a classic. I know it's not Psalms. I found the New Testament book to be more readable, starting with Matthew, Mark, Luke, and John. Don't expect me to remember any of that either. I think now, that if I had found a nice congregation at that time, things would have been different.

I went to a car dealer named Tony in southeast Portland and traded straight across my car for a 1965 brown Ford F-150 pickup. This was probably one of the best vehicle investments I made at that time. I rarely drove it. I parked it near a park with most of my stuff covered by a tarp in the bed, of the truck. The rest of the time I was on foot. My mission to survive. Yes, it was all about survival, weathering the elements, when to eat, where to crap. Decisions, decisions to make during those below zero nights. I would find empty apartments with working electricity. Lucky, I had my backpack. I could shower and shave. In the mornings, I would sometimes steal someone's bag of cans and cash them in for donuts. I was proud of one thing. I didn't drink alcohol or do any drugs the whole two years I was homeless.

When I truly was homeless the weather was not accommodating. The winter was below zero with the wind chill factor. I walked everywhere to keep warm. I wore long johns, thick socks, my heavy jacket, and my back pack, and a hoodie. I walked down by the river, and saw nutria strewn all over the river banks. The nutria was frozen solid. Nutria are large rodents that look like beavers with a long rat tail, ugly creatures to say the least.

As I continued to walk in the early evening, I saw a Texaco station with a light on. I went to it. The door was open, nobody was there. I think there was a cash register there. I didn't look. I was hungry. There was a stand with nuts and other assorted packed stuff. I helped myself and left. Eventually I wore holes in my shoes. Lucky, I had another pair so I could keep moving. I discovered that sometimes to survive is to make do. Yes, I do believe that God helps those who help themselves, but only when necessary.

Eventually I got tired of living like this. I called home. Mom answered and said, "Why do you always call us?" Finally, Dad got on the line and said he would meet with me. Dad and I did meet. It was like looking at spitting images of ourselves. Dad was forthright and to the point. He said either you seek counseling, or I have to let you go. Having to choose between those alternatives, I chose counseling. I was sick and didn't know what it was. Turns out, five years with one Psychiatrist later, it was determined that I have Bipolar Disorder/Manic Depressive. The first Meds I took were Prozac.

As it turned out I longshored when available. I paid Mom rent and worked around the house. I also showed the American Foreign-Exchange (AFS) High School students around at times. Mom and Dad did host a couple of these students. It was a learning experience for us as much as it was for them.

Casino

The Mill Casino in Coos Bay/North Bend became my main employer for almost two years as a valet. It was a good enough job with benefits and one week vacation a year. Thank you, Coquille Indian tribe. You all gave me the opportunity to go back to school. I got accepted by the University of Idaho for their Recreation program at 37 years of age.

University of Idaho

The University of Idaho (U of I) excursion proved to me I could still get passing grades in a Recreation program with straight C's which included Abnormal Psychology and Medical terminology. Schooling at Moscow, Idaho, was very expensive. The weather was so much different than Coos Bay. The weather would vary from snowy to sunny every day. The air there was crisp. A lungful of air there was so refreshing. There were different activities like mountain climbing, skiing, canoeing and hiking. I ended up in the best shape of my life there, walking to the food dorm from my graduate-campus room in the Alumnae building, walking to class, walking to eat, and doing exercise classes. I was logging in 10+ miles a day. The University of Idaho's mascot is the Vandals, another word for Viking. It was fun, a great atmosphere to go to school. Also, it was near the big school in Pullman, home of Washington State University. One could always hang out there.

Finding a job in Portland

After a term at the University of Idaho, I went to Portland looking for a job in the field. Through the Oregon State employment service, I got a job at the airport as a Transportation Assistant (TA). The most haunting thing that happened to me was receiving a phone call from a Supervisor. He told me to turn on my T.V. It was 9/11. It was hard to believe; however, it indeed was real.

As a TA, I saw and met a number of star athletes, politicians, celebrities, and local celebrities. The former Blazer, Maurice Lucas to me was the single most super athlete that I met in PDX. It happened during a Hawaiian return flight. I was talking to one of the security guards and noticed Maurice walking by and told the guard. Now Maurice was a big tall guy. The guard was only slightly smaller. The guard walked up to Lucas and said, "Maurice Lucas." Lucas turned fast and said, "Yah," sort of aggravated. The guard said, "Can I have your autograph?" In a meek voice Maurice smiled and signed his little notepad. After that, he surprised me by walking up to me and asking me what my name was. So, I told him, and he repeated it to himself. Then he said, "I see you around." I told Luke that he still looked in playing shape. He replied, "Only half court nowadays." That was a real cool memory.

Another guy who passed through the roadways was Jean Claude Van Damme, the martial artist. We bumped into each other. I saw he was a short guy like myself. He knew what he was doing. Also, where he was going.

I was working by the computer one day, while Senator Gordon Smith was waiting for his ride. Other personalities I met include Marv Albert, Dennis Erickson, Danny Glover, Steve Jones, John Kitzhaber, Lee Ann Rhymes, and many more.

I had worked awhile at the Airport and I found myself stewing over some things I didn't like. I don't know what set me off. But I do know this much: The Airport transportation assistant job was messing with my life clock, and that job was a complete dead end for me. I felt trapped and wanted to get out of there. I got a call from them on my day off telling me to come in. I did, reluctantly. When I got to the airport I was in and out of there real fast. I wasn't friendly about it. I walked up to the Computer Relay and Airport Communication booth. I had my name tag access card in hand; bombed it through the open window and yelled, "Take it." Then I left for good.

It was night and I still had a lot to go through. I went back to my apartment, put on my hooded Miami Dolphins jacket, picked up my biggest wood baseball bat and went back to the airport. I drove through the area that was free access and parked by the building I knew I could get into. Once again, I made fast work of it. Entering the building I made straight for the phone on the wall. I blasted the phone, and wall three times. It came tumbling out of the wall. I left knowing there was no camera looking over me.

I took off to my brother's house. When I got to Kane's place, he was home. He looked at my hand and noticed it was bleeding. He tended to my hand, hydrogen peroxide, ointment, and a good loose bandage wrap. One small part of the wound was near the bone. I told Kane all that happened so far. He listened. If I remember correctly Mom and Dad were in Melbourne, Florida caring for my German aunt in her waning moments. They had left their car at Kane's. I told Kane that I wanted to go to Coos Bay. I asked for mom's car. He handed me the key. Why I wanted to go there I don't remember. After I left Kane's place, I went back to my place, put on some warm clothes, long johns, heavy jeans, and comfortable Romeo slip-on shoes. Then I took off for Coos Bay.

I was cruising at a pretty fast speed to take care of some personal business at the home front in Coos Bay (so I thought!). I was just past Albany on Interstate 5, when the car started floating. I pulled over to the side of the road. The Honda had run out of gas. I never once looked at the gas gauge when I took off. It now was on E. Now I was on foot walking down the Freeway at a good pace. I can only guess how far I went before a State trooper pulled me over. He was a tall lanky guy with big hands. He went through the police routine with me. I explained that my car had ran out of gas further back up the freeway. So, he took me to a gas station. He took out a two-gallon gas can that was in his car. We had it filled and went back to the Honda and put in the two gallons of gas. He waited until I got the car started and then he left. I went to a gas station, filled up, and was on my way again. I went down the freeway and cut off at Highway 38. On my way to my territorial stomping grounds - Coos Bay-North Bend. When I got to the North Bend Bridge, I drove over it. I found the town to be so typically foggy and quiet. It was so early in the morning. Driving up the hill I was looking forward to some rest at the house. When I approached the driveway, I saw the big Cadillac, which was the car that Dad had found for Luhia, my cousin Danny's daughter from the Big Island of Hawaii (Hilo). She was on the mainland to attend Southwestern Oregon Community College. She was going to school and playing volleyball. I cursed myself for not remembering a house key. I knocked a couple of times on the front door. I waited a short while, then left back to Portland.

I was speeding back to Portland from the start. When I came to the curve of the Reedsport water reservoir, I floored it. The car was whipping around the curve. The steering wheel went one way while I tried to pull it the other way. The car flipped in the air and landed, crashing in the middle of Highway 101. I had some sort of out-of-body experience. I still don't know if I believe it. But I'm still here to talk about it. It was all sort of like slow motion. I remember being somehow in the air watching myself, looking at the crash. Then suddenly being back in my own body seeing the real crash. The car was totaled. Full airbag deployment is probably what saved me. I don't know. All I had as signs of the crash were a seatbelt strap burn and a few scrapes. While I was beside the car a hand touched my shoulder and directed me to a big box ambulance. I suddenly noticed a line of traffic, from the South side, and the North side. Than I was off to the Reedsport Hospital. When I got there on a gurney the nurse asked me about next of family. I gave her Kane's phone number and shortly after that passed out. When Kane got there, I was in a hospital bed with a drip, line and needle taped to my arm. Kane was his same old "Stare you down" self. I guess that I would be sort of angry too in the circumstances. I was woke up to go to Reedsport. We must have been there a while because it was light outside. No words were spoken accept for my little quips. We went to our neighbor's house for lunch. It was quite a manic episode, from Airport to there. After that, I don't remember much.

My brother Kane quit casual Longshoring, seeing it as a dead end. He got a job, through his friend Tom Ward, in Portland and was staying with the Wards in Lake Oswego. Kane ended up being called to work in Sacramento working. Since I was barely working as a casual longshoreman myself, I helped Kane by moving his stuff down there. I stayed with Kane each time I brought his stuff down. I really liked Sacramento. Kane's place was situated in the middle of everything. I ended up working five days as an

Spending a moment with the bear at the California border, on the way to Sacramento.

unidentified casual longshoreman there. The port, and the hiring hall were small for the size of the area. They exported logs, rice, fertilizer, when I was there. Sacramento was fun too.

Fun Times on the Path

Rose Bowl
The grand-daddy of bowl games was finally going to be played by the Oregon Ducks going against the powerful Nittany Lions of Penn State. I ordered two tickets, but, once again, ended up going solo. I was supposed to meet a friend from high school there. Her name is Katherine. Either we crossed paths, or she just didn't show. I searched the area in the coliseum where she said she would be. Spectators during halftime were looking at me. I said I'm looking for someone. They replied, "We can see that." Before the game started, I took in the Rose Bowl Parade. There were many beautiful and interesting floats, horses, and more things to see. That took up all my morning before the game. Parking was great at the game, a huge meadow for parking.

I traded my tickets for one 40-yard line seat. It was worth it I could survey the whole field. As the game started, Penn State ran the opening kickoff for a touchdown. I thought it was going to be a blow out, but the Ducks hung in there. They went into the half with the lead. During halftime, just before I was looking for Katherine, some guy in front of me said, "Hey!" I just had bumped into Ahmad Rashad, Oregon's great running back from the 1970's. Sure enough, there he was wearing his letterman's jacket strolling on to where ever. Oregon ended up losing the game. As Penn State tried to run up the score the Ducks were respectable! I stayed with family down in Pasadena. It was nice to see them all, then go do my thing. It was fun!

Mr. Volunteer
In Coos Bay Mr. Volunteer was me for a while and believe you me that really does suck. You do things that are supposedly good for the community. You suddenly have all these so-called friends. For example, I ran for City Council. I pulled in several votes, good considering there were only three signs posted, one by the wood chip pile Highway 101. With three openings to be elected, I came in fourth in the voting. So, I signed on to become a Firefighter. Quite frankly, it was a duty of being available for a couple days and on call. Six months later I was done with it; quite probably bi-polar disorder had something to do with it. Finally, I ended the volunteerism on a good note by being selected by former teacher Gus Langley (deceased) to be on the tree committee. I completed my term and ended on a good note with all of it.

On to Europe
Casual Longshoring was slow and I had saved some money to make the trip to Europe a lucrative one. I went solo, which suited me better. I flew out of Seattle to Germany

via Lufthansa. The flight was packed and crowded as expected. Nothing special about the long flight other than it got me from point A to point B. When I arrived, I was greeted by Ulla, an aunt and her son Lutz; whom I had met before in Coos Bay. I went to Lutz's place, in an apartment in Berlin, a small place yet quaint, way high up. I met Lutz's fiancée, Svetlanna. She was a very nice young lady, nineteen or twenty years old at the time. She had a prosthetic leg. Yet all that aside, she was a Russian doll, very kind and sweet. Lutz was always off to work.

I determined that it was time to leave and check out the rest of Europe. I had a buddy from high school, and college waiting for me in Baumholder, just south of Frankfurt and not that far from Kaiserslauten (K-town). My friend Chet Mackey was waiting at the Frankfurt train station. As I was pulling in, I saw Chet holding his little boy Derrick. I met Chet's wife Hey Suk, who was expecting with another boy. Chet was a captain in the Army at the time. It was good to see him. Chet, Derrick, and I took an hour-long cruise down the Rhein River. It was very nice. It included going by the Lorelei, steep slate rock on the right bank of the Rhine Gorge. Supposedly there was a sad folktale that went with that place. We also went to Trier which had a Roman coliseum, which I believe was for battles of one form or another, and other ruins. We sped down the Autobahn where there is no speed limit. Chet had a nice quaint place. But man, it was hot at that time when I went to that part of Germany. The visit was very nice. Chet and I go way back so that added to the trip.

The next stop on my agenda was Hamburg. Chet asked me, "What's in Hamburg?" I told him, "Hamburgers," which gave him a chuckle. I was off to Hamburg on the Eurail. The trip there was fast and nice. Hamburg was a beautiful city. I found a hostel in no time through my Go Europe book/guide. The place was comfortable and cheap. If you wanted a beer, just go to the vending machine. I must have put my footprints all over Hamburg, only stopping to eat and drink.

I jumped on the next train to Munich, which was a little bit longer trip. I met a guy at the rail station. He asked me my name, so I told him. He said. "Klaus, that's Italian." That was perplexing until I remembered there was this guy, named Klaus Dibiassi, who was an Olympic Gold medalist in diving for Italy -interesting. Anyway, I spent near a week at a campsite. I rented a tent and slept the whole time. I needed it.

When I finally got out of hibernation, I jumped onto the next train for Salzburg. Beautiful country. I don't remember what I did there, but I do remember the beauty. The mountains, trees - this was the start of Austria. I have fond memories of taking the Tram, up and down. What a view! My next stop was Innsbruck.

From there I went to Zurich, Switzerland. There were nice cobblestone roads and an old man with a music box, having his dressed monkey collect money from the tourists. Not sure where I stayed or what I did for food there.

After my stay in Zurich, I jumped the train for Bern. When in Bern I took a taxi to a hotel which was not cheap. In most all these countries I stayed in youth hostels. The reason I spent up was mostly because I needed a room with a phone. A good family friend back home, Carl Granich, had given me the number of a French girl by the name of Michele. Meeting Michele would have been nice. I wanted to go to France and take in the food, and sights there. I called her in the evening. We had a long conversation. There was simply no way to meet. We wished each other well. That was the end of the conversation.

After a good night's sleep and breakfast, I was once again on the Eurail, this time to Lichtenstein. The smallest country in the world, Lichtenstein was beautiful. Vaduz, the capitol, had lots of green grass, and was surrounded by the Alps. I stayed in a pink youth hostel there. It was huge. I still had my eyes set on France for a visit. It was just a hop, skip, and a jump to Nice, France.

I met three Turkish guys, all of them told me that if you can't speak the French language don't go there. I took their word for it. The next day I was off. My next stop was Milan, Italy. The sights in and around Milan were nothing but desert, which explains why the popular spaghetti westerns in the day flourished. I only had a four hour stop in Milan. I enjoyed a big plate of spaghetti and moved along to Venice.

When we approached Venice, I saw that it was raining cats and dogs. Instead of getting soaked, I got on a water taxi, and went to a hostel that had space available. Venice was OK, but it was a little too romantic for me. After all I was solo. All said and done, so far, I was running through Europe fast. I could have spent the rest of my time and money in Italy -the history, architecture, art, and cathedrals. This would have been overwhelming.

Unfortunately, I had to move on. I had a lot of places to go and not a lot of time, or so I thought. I left Italy and went back to Austria, Vienna to be exact. Vienna was nice too - high mountains, and wonderful blue cloudy skies. There were no places available to sleep. Fortunately, a lady flagged me down. She asked me if I needed a room, to which I immediately responded, "Yes." The room turned out to be a Pension by her house. This suited me just fine. It wasn't very expensive. That night I went to a nearby Inn. What I wanted was some meat and potatoes. What I got was a big bowl of spaghetti.

After an uneventful night I went to sleep. The next morning, I took a taxi to the train station. I decided that I would go to Czechoslovakia, Prague to be exact. Prague would prove to be that historic place

> I don't know if it's true or not, but I discovered my name Klaus means "Victory of the people". It carries some responsibility. My mother heard this and exclaimed, "Powerful." My brother Kane was on the internet and found Klaus in the Greek version citing "Nikos" Nicolas, or St. Nick (Santa Klaus!) All interesting to say the least.

I hadn't encountered yet - horse carriages in the middle of the city and large buildings with huge working clocks. I stayed in a small hotel for a few days, the Juventus, where the most expensive dish was ham and eggs. It was nice, quaint, and I enjoyed it.

When I left Prague, I was ready to go back to Germany. I returned happy and content about my trip so far. We landed in East Germany, so I had to figure which subway, the U bahn or the S bahn, went to the west side. I found out, cruised into West Berlin and got off at my stop. It was evening when I returned to West Berlin. I stopped at Lutz's place. He let me in, and we talked awhile. Then I went to sleep. Lutz went to work the next morning. Svetlanna being a haus-frau stayed home. The next day, I met mom's cousin Manfred Wolf and his wife Elfie both middle-aged and so very nice. The day was beautiful. Manfred suggested we go through the Spreewald, which was a series of river canals that had stops. This was traveled by a long canoe, with a guide. This trip was noted for its specialty - a dill pickle stop.

I was really satisfied with my European experience. That was until I got home. Work was nil to none. I could have spent another month in Europe. Coming home was a waste of time.

Past catches up in Bandon

I went to Bandon, for the helluvit. It ended up with me getting arrested for trespassing in a store called the Jewelry Thief. The police officer taking me to Coquille to get booked. He had a big German shepherd sitting by me in the car. I had a thought and spoke German to the dog, and he immediately began licking my face (so friendly). The dog's trainer-boss was not happy with the turn of events, however. He said, "Be Quiet."

Now I must tell you this. It was about three years after I left that Airport job. I got a phone call from the Airport Police. The officer turned out to be a small blonde. It took a long while, but they had the evidence that it was me who did the damage to the phone, and wall. The Bandon/Coos County fingerprints nailed me. I would eventually make three installments to pay off the damage. When I agreed to the payments the officer said, "All

Andre Barber with me on deck a ship we were working on.

we want to know is why you did it." When I wouldn't answer, she said, "You just wanted to get to them before they got to you." I said, "Yep!" We walked out of the Dairy Queen. She was licking her ice cream cone.

Betty Ford Center

During my eighth year on the job as a registered longshoreman, I was starting to take my job for granted. I would always go to work and do my job. But then after work I would be isolated which led to trouble for me. I went out to bars, did drugs, and frolicked with illicit women, all for some false sense of companionship. Fortunately, I never had a tangle with the law at that time.

One day I went to our Dispatch hall. A fellow longshoreman came up to me. He said, "Klaus, your losing weight." That night I went home and looked in the mirror. He was right, I looked like a drug addict. First thing the next morning I called Brian Harvey, our drug and alcohol representative. I knew Brian from way back. He is a brother, and one of my better friends. We talked. The next day, I was off to Palm Springs to the Betty Ford Center (BFC). Brian dropped me off at the Portland airport, where I boarded the plane to Palm Springs. When I landed, I was picked up by a chauffeur and taken to the BFC. There I was greeted by some wonderful people - Staff, counselors, and such.

I was at the Center for ninety days. During that experience I learned about Alcoholics Anonymous. Imagine that - 45 years old, and I hadn't heard of AA? There were doctors, lawyers, airplane pilots, influential businessmen, actors, you name it with me, all afflicted with the disease of addiction. This was the first place where I learned the Serenity prayer. I still cherish it. The steps are what we were all there for. There are twelve. I worked my way up to the seventh step before I went back to Portland. When I was done at the BFC I had made a lot of male compadres, also a few women, because we went to meetings together. It was that way at the BFC -the housing for men and women were separate. This makes sense, doesn't it? The last thing I will mention about the BFC is this. I lived in a building by the name of DuPont. Mel Gibson has his brick laid in front of the building, making me think that he might have been there at one time.

Sobriety

Back in Portland Brian picked me up and took me to my condo. We talked about sober living and that I should find such a place to help regulate my already mounting mania of bi-polar disorder. Medication was and is necessary. Then Brian told me I had a sponsor which was Kurt Milspa, whom I'd already knew. I found a place to live called Serenity Homes. They had a few houses and I lived in the Nevada house. It was in that house during a meeting where I met my good friend, Kenny Douglas. He is my best friend now.

One early evening, in the late fall I was off my meds for a while. I had gotten into a manic cycle. Peter, a kid in the house, was pushing my buttons and making me highly volatile. Needless to say, I scared him bad. I had to leave the house in order to maintain peace. The problem was that I had no money, and no place to go. I called a so-called friend at the time and he told me to sleep in the park. My temper was growing. I mean, I paid big rent money to have a room in that Nevada street house just to be told to go. As it turned out in by mid-day, I was at my ropes end. The owner of the House of Serenity told me the night before to leave the house (but leave your shit!). There was a big target on him from one mad Hawaiian. I went to his residence, kicked in his front door with a bare foot. It only took one kick and the door exploded inward off the hinges. I saw him hiding behind a bunch of pillows and roughed him up a little bit. He ran away. I left and then turned myself in to the police. Now I was on my own.

Running a forklift as a longshoreman.

I ended up making plenty of amends after my stay at the Betty Ford Center. For instance, I put my brother through hell by having him take care of my stuff in Oregon while I was gone in Palm Springs. It also backfired on me. I ended up back in jail. Yet I persevered through that jail mess, yet again. I learned to think through my amends, then sincerely approach and apologize for the wrong I felt that I had done. This felt good when it worked. Step 10 of how it works is in the Big Blue Book on page 158. It tells us that when we have an immediate problem to automatically make amends and move on. This is my favorite step of the 12 steps. There are times when I fuck up! So, to make amends on them is huge. Now I carry a 24-hour coin on my key chain. It reminds me each day sober is a good day, or at least a sober day.

Merk

There was the time when I was at the right place at the right time to help get a new U.S. Senator elected into office - Senator Jeff Merkley Democrat for Oregon. That was back in 2008. I had heard that the Merkley campaign needed extra's for a Promo. Through Shelby, our ILWU Secretary, I learned that Dawn of Local 40 was helping with Jeff's campaign. I called Dawn, and she told me where the Promo was going to be - in an old dilapidated building in Linnton, Oregon, just north of Portland on Highway 30. Dawn said to be there at a certain time.

I had other ideas. The day before the camera crew was to come and set up for the shoot, I went to the old Linnton Mill to find out the history of it. The inside was a dark, aged place, with old machinery covered in dust and spider webs. The place was huge. I walked way to the back of the mill. There, I saw a partially opened door. I knocked on the door. An older big man opened the door. His name was Archie. He was the owner of this Mill. When I met Archie, I found out he liked to talk as much as I did. He was as friendly as they come. We talked way into the early evening before I left. I told Archie that I would be back early the next day. He acknowledged that. His cat followed him to the door. I was back plenty early and was ready to meet Jeff and wish him best of luck. After all, he was going up against a strong incumbent in Gordon Smith. Archie and I were conversing.

When it was about 2 or 3 o'clock, I heard a slight brushing sound on the inside of the building. I told Archie they were here. Archie said he never heard a thing. We went out. There was a catered long table with food and drink. I asked Archie what he wanted. He said, "Coffee" so I got him some java brew. He later told me that was the best coffee he ever had. That made me happy. All of three, or four of us were told that they wanted facial shots, in short mug shots of us. I had to get a little make-up put on by a specialist named Crystal. Than I was put under a light, while sitting on a chair looking forward. The whole process took about five minutes. After that was done, I saw Jeff talking to three Longshoremen, two checkers, and a boss. Just as they left, I walked up to him and started talking with Jeff. I had to stand on a box for a picture sequence that showed us communicating eye to eye. I never once got residuals or pictures that was promised to me by Ben, one of the coordinators. As it turned out, I went to the long table and got some food and left through a door that Archie was holding open for me. So Cool! As the politics continued during his campaign, my facial mug shot was shown on many intervals of programming on television all over the state, almost four months as a political ad promo. I saw it once. That was enough. Some of my fellow workers said, "You're famous." What could I do but glow and say, "Nah?" Merkley won by the slimmest of margins. I think he is a good man for us and for the state of Oregon.

Still figuring it out

Somebody told me, "Take care of your own self." I did. I couldn't afford my own lawyer. So, guess what. I had to do the time.

A quick comment our public defenders. They suck, but only because they are overloaded with cases.

There are some brothers I would like to thank for their efforts on my behalf during this time: Bruce Holte, for a supportive letter about me and my work ethics. Kurt Milspa wrote a letter about being my sponsor. Brian Harvey went up on the stand with me, and we were shaking in our boots. When the woman-judge said. "I don't care if you ever work again." I believe she was just about to throw away the key away on me. When I bowed my head, she knew I had given her the respect she wanted.

Jail time sucked. I endured it, and then I went to a sober house called Homeward Bound. I also had to do anger management. It was completed in six months. After one month in Homeward Bound, Kenny Douglas joined us. I left Homeward Bound after six months. Kenny left a month later. Than we came together again.

New York

Margaret and Pete Ward led us on the sports tour in New York.

After the Merkley promo, in fact the very next day, I was on a flight to New York City to watch the Yankee's play baseball. It would be their last season in the old Yankee Stadium, something very special. I got a flyer from Tom Ward, a Portland Longshoreman like myself. I contacted Tom's dad Pete, a former Major league player, and paid him to be part of a sports tour, which turned out to be a lot of fun.

It was a three-game series versus the Boston Red Sox. Before we flew out of PDX. I met the immediate Ward family - Margaret, Pete's wife; Mike, the oldest son; Steve the middle son; and Tom, the youngest. On this trip I will say everyone was real cordial, and nice in our group. I met Marlin Grahn. He was Portland State University's former wrestling coach. There was Cap, and his grandson Conner, John, and others that I don't recollect.

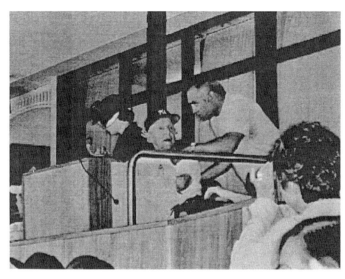

At the announcer's booth at Yankee Stadium.

New York seemed to fit me like a glove. I got along with everyone. I really liked the sights, the sounds, the smells; and that everything was happening 24 hours/ 7 days a week. We were staying at the Marriot in downtown Manhattan, about eighty stories high. The rooms were immaculate, and the service was top of the line. It was a real modern classy place to stay. I loved the Marriot. Those elevators seemed like giant rockets. Going up some great height.

From the beginning this was not a cheap trip. My roommate on the trip was a guy named Jeff Selby, a nice guy! He had called me prior to the flight and asked me if I would like to go to the live showing of the David Letterman show. That was fine with me. The first guest on Dave's show was a lady comedian. She was good. The next guest was the sultry Kim Kardashian. She's just another pretty face to look at (so I thought at the time). The final guest was another comedian. He was good too. The night before Jeff and I had dinner at Shula's steak house where I ordered Porterhouse steaks for the both of us. When the meal came, I had a glass of Merlot wine with it. I covered the cost for both of our dinners. The next day I was having breakfast near my room. The waiter was as nice as they come. So, I gave him a good tip. He then offered me two tickets to see a Broadway Theatre showing of "Gypsy." I took them. Not knowing

what to do with them I gave them to John, one of our bunch. What he did with those tickets I will never know.

Before any of the baseball games were played, we did a tour of the Stadium. We checked out the Hall of Fame and the upper stands where the announcers were supposed to be. It was an excellent tour. There were a lot of pictures taken.

After the first game, when we left the stadium the first time, we went back to the Hotel where I did one of the things that I do best -shopping! I still to this day have clothes, signs, small bats etc. from New York. I also lost a lot of stuff on the way back. I was so excited about the first game - my hotdog and soda were the best thing. Boston smashed us.

The next game was a day later so I just took in that part of New York. I was heading back to the room when I ran into the security guard. He was cool. He asked me if I wanted a pair of NFL preseason football tickets - Patriots vs. Giants. He said he couldn't go so he was giving them away. I told him that I would have taken them graciously, but I was going to Brooklyn to watch the Yankee's play. Once again, the Yankee's lost to the Red Sox. It wasn't even close. We took the subway back to the Marriot. I went looking around and did some shopping.

Finally, it was the last game of the series. The Yankee's won on a bases loaded homer by a big-name player, Jason Giambi. The

My nephew Koa with me at Longshoreman Hall in front of art piece of a hand with a grappling hook.

crowd left happy and satisfied. The very next day the tour group went to Yogi Berra's museum. It was cool! I ended up purchasing a baseball there that had one of his quotes on it. The quote said. "It ain't over till it's over." I gave the ball to my nephew Koa. On the way home we took the bus back to the airport, just how we had come in. We were back in New Jersey, Newark to fly out, as we had flown in. I don't remember the length of the flight. But it was similar as before. The whole New York visit was perfect as far as weather was concerned. It was a good trip. I thought it was great. This trip fulfilled my ideas about New York City big time.

Back home in Portland I had a deaf girlfriend, who had two teenage girls. Turns out that Meg never really did like me. I didn't see the whole picture until I almost fell into a house deal that I could never get out from under no thanks to her. Fortunately, I was able to get out of it.

I had a wild whim one night. I decided to donate all my loose change (which was considerable) to the Duck wrestling program which was on the fritz. I ended up having three doubled up store bags, each practically full of assorted change. I boxed it up and wrote the Athletic department on it and my former coach's name, Ron Finley, now deceased. I only did this because I thought that wrestling at U of O might have a chance.

I had no idea that there would be a rub off of sports. Wrestling was the one that had to go. This was all done prior to me sending off my money. To continue with my grandiose idea with the box of money, I sent it to the Athletic Dept. via freight. It cost me twenty dollars to do that. About a week later Coach Finley called me and said there was a big hoopla going on about the package. People were taking pictures of it and such. The media had caught wind of it. A lady from one of the news stations called. Her name was Michele. She asked, "Why did you just give the money away?" I mentioned that it was a donation to keep the wrestling program at Oregon. Deep inside, I knew that wasn't going to happen soon, if at all.

As far as sports go in Eugene, I might take in a track and field meet when I can. After all Eugene is track town USA. What could be better?

U of O again

In early September of 2012, my girlfriend (later my wife) and I decided we would take in a Duck football game. The game was the first of the season, UofO vs. Arkansas St. It was the debut of former Duck quarterback Marcus Mariota. We can call this our walking spree from start to almost the end. First, we drove down to Eugene, did some window shopping in down town and then I parked way behind the dormitories, free parking. We walked to campus and checked out my old dorm, Carson. Then we walked through campus to the Duck bookstore. After that we started our walk to Autzen stadium. We stopped to eat. When it was close to game time we walked, then waited in line to get into the stadium. Once inside I found us our seats, very good ones with cushiony seats. As the stadium filled up the game was about to begin. At the start, Marcus had some problems. At the half UofO had an insurmountable lead. We left, walking back. We were close to the car when my girlfriend sat on a bench and said; "go get the car and pick me up." She was plumb walked out. The whole thing was fun, to the end.

Salmon Fishing

During the summer of 2013 Kenny and I went on our second trip for salmon. The first time was on the Willamette River. This time we were camping out in the small town of Chinook, Washington. We were fishing on Gary Douglas's boat, Kenny's dad. We camped out in the evening. We put in early in the morning. We fished by buoy 10, in the Columbia River. This was the first day. All three of us caught our limit. Kenny landed a 30lb Chinook full of eggs. We enjoyed baked salmon that night.

The next day was interesting to say the least. We put in early again. The wind was up past noon and the water was choppy. Plenty of boats dotted the

A successful fishing day with Kenny

Columbia River and there was an unusual amount of sea lions. The sea lions coated the buoys, and heads popped up everywhere. Kenny had hooked a salmon. He ended up reeling in a salmon head. The body viciously taken by a sea lion. A short while later I hooked one. The fish took my line way out, so I had a fight on my hands. I reeled and it would go back out to sea over and over again. Finally, we saw the fish jump. It was a big Chinook. I tried to get it close to the boat. He went straight back out again. When I did get him to the boat Gary had the net in the water while Kenny was steering the boat. This fish was a big one. Gary was just about to net it when suddenly this huge monstrous head

Just a note: Did you know Kalama, in Washington is Hawaiian. It means "garden" in Hawaiian. The name is such because the Hawaiians used to navigate the waterways for the Indians. Who would've thought it?

appeared out of the water - a big sea lion. It took the fish from the net. Poor Gary was maybe two feet from the thing. I was cussing up a storm. That sea lion took my salmon and all the rigging on my pole. Talk about being pissed off!

A Snow Storm Adventure in Portland.

The snow in Portland was bad enough to cause wrecks, and leave vehicles empty, and stranded along many freeways, highways, and streets. I was on my way to work, driving along Highway 30, when all hell broke loose on me near the St. John's Bridge. A car was slowing down in front of me. I hit a slick spot and veered right. I went with the veer and tried to straighten out so I could get back on the main road. That didn't happen. Instead, my truck continued to go right fast. I smashed into a sign, blasting it into oblivion. I then found myself in the middle of the railroad tracks. Coming to my senses, I put my truck in 4-wheel 4 high drive. I bounced off the tracks and back into on-coming traffic. I was still out of control. Luckily for me, the on-coming traffic stopped. The left-hand lane stopped too, as I regained control of my truck. I learned a valuable lesson that day. In snow always keep it in 4-wheel drive. When I got to work, I couldn't believe it. There were two little dents on the front driver's side door, and a few scrapes. God was looking after me. I do believe that. One of my sandbags flew out of the bed of my pick-up. I'm sure it was when I was bouncing on the railroad tracks. Later in the work day my friend Butch told me about some guy who did what I just wrote about. I admitted that it was me. Later another longshoreman, Rich, told me he witnessed the whole thing. He eventually walked away. In leaving he called me a crazy son-of-a-bitch. I must admit that I love that truck. I bought it from Tim Rosenbloom of Tim's Automotive & Repair.

Getting trucks loaded on to the ship as a boss.

Sports Tour

A couple years ago, I think mid-October, my wife booked a sports tour for me. She didn't want to go so I went solo. The game was football. It was a dream of mine. It was also on my Bucket List. The Miami Dolphins, my "favorite team" versus the always tough Pittsburg Steelers. I flew out of Portland to Fort Lauderdale. When there, I did a lot, too much to remember. I did do some collecting down there. I have a sports card, and memorabilia collection. I added some down there in Miami. When at the game I did quite a lot, then found my seat. It was between two girl Steeler fans. They were very nice. I always heard opposing fans were gruff and rowdy. This was just not so, at least not in Miami. I saw Don Shula on the big screens, as well as Dan Marino. He was in the middle of the field talking to the Steelers Quarterback Big Ben Rothlisberger, all three football legends, Shula, and Marino both Hall of Famers. The game itself was great from the start. I thought Pittsburg was going to blow us out of the water. We came back and won. What a thrill that was.

Gregg Patton

Gregg is a fellow Longshoreman. I met my friend Gregg Patton close to my house. He was driving us to Eugene to see the UofO Ducks play the UofW Huskies. The Huskies were ranked 5th in the country. The Ducks were ranked 19th. It would be a big win for either team. When we got to Eugene, we had a flat tire, by luck near a Goodyear tire store. We walked a good one and a half miles through downtown, through campus, and over the trail to Autzen stadium. We had lunch there. The place was just crawling with people. The game itself was a semi-high scoring affair with the Ducks winning in overtime 37 to 34. The game was a lot of fun. Especially winning in the end.

Art

Piece I did in the 7th Grade.

I love Art. It is profound that I find I'm fairly good with artwork and its mediums. As a youngster I won awards under the tutelage of Earl Schnoor (deceased). I received many blue-ribbon awards. My first money award was $25 for a conservation picture in the 6th grade. As I went through high school and college I fiddled with my artwork, but not seriously. I painted fire scenes in a warehouse and on a support beam and built a float for the Curry County Fair.

I took art classes when I graduated from high school, at South-western Oregon Community College in Coos Bay. I took drawing and print-making there. Again, I shined in my artwork for athletics, wrestling, and track at SWOCC.

When I met my wife in June 2011, I had an inkling to do artwork again. My creative juices and ideas came back to me. I took a course at the Northwest College of Arts in the Pearl District on how to make comic books. I succeeded with a comic I called "The Wave." I made and gave away about fifty copies I had printed. In short, the story is about a surfing experience that could have been fatal.

I have painted about 15 cross-saws and 10 circular saws, each having its own flair. I got paid for two. Of the others, only some I know found good homes. I did one canvas painting of a beach scene. I know this has a good home. Brian Harvey says he always gets comments about it.

My pride and joy is at the Mt. Park Recreation Center. It is a 110 lb. piece of cast iron plate design with a large wave scene that is painted on it. The artwork is mounted on a wall, facing a large window that the stationary bikes are behind. My cousin Charlie, who must be something of an art critic told me that in Oregon that piece is worth $25,000 and in New York $50,000. I was in awe! It was a donation (gift) to the facility.

One piece of artwork is at my old high school (Marshfield), in Coos Bay. It is a 7' band saw blade 8" wide with an undersea world scene on it. My friend Brian Trendell, School Superintendent, and his secretary Peggy liked the saw. They will put it in a

good place. The kids in the woodshop are supposedly building a frame for it. I guess I'll hear about it when that's done. By the way, Brian still calls me "Gator."

One final piece I am extremely proud of is a 2' circular blade, in which I had the holes filled in by Brian Correll. He did it like a cinnamon roll, outside to in. That was the mettle of that blade. What I did was a piece of cake with Bigfoot walking toward the forest on the backside and a Sasquatch scene on the front. Surreal to say the least. This blade went to a friend, Jeff Perry. He really wanted this done.

I also paint designs on planters, be it for the yard, fence, or wall. It's all good.

Sports Idols

I had all kinds of sports idols growing up. Muhammad Ali had to be the most popular. OJ Simpson had a big fan during my youth along with the perfect 17-0 Miami Dolphins, with that no-name defense. Baseball is and will always be Babe Ruth. If I had to pick a pitcher; it would be Nolan Ryan. Today's basketball stars have such monstrous personalities like LeBron James, such great talent Dr. J was a personal favorite. Oh, I left out Air Jordan.

Meadowlark Lemon autographed the pair of sweats I won in a raffle the day of their performance!

Prefontaine

On to a truly memorable event, what I remember as the Steve Prefontaine Invite versus Finland and, hopefully, the great Lasse Viren who was the current Olympic Champion. Viren never did show, But Steve did. It was all happening in Coos Bay at the Marshfield High School track where Pre was a legend. The meet also included Mac Wilkins, the current Olympic Champion in the discus. I must have been 11 or 12 years of age at the time. It was a total thrill just to see so many good, and great athletes there.

Dad and I were watching high in the top bleachers of what is now Pete Susick stadium. The rest of the family was down below somewhere, ready to see the track and field event live. Pre, the runner, was like a fine-tuned racecar. His warm-ups alone must have been 45 minutes or longer. This included stretching, etc. After the race, his warm-down was just as long. But before I get ahead of myself, there was the race. I think the race was 2000 meters. I'm not sure about that. Whatever it was, Pre was intense; and a strict runner. His typical style was "All Out!" After all, he was our hometown hero. He would prove no less. The race was over when it started. Pre just showed us all why he was so great. He even lapped some runners to boot. When it was over Pre had set another record. He took a couple victory laps, as much show, as it was a warm-down. It was a totally satisfied crowd. As kids surrounded Pre for his autograph, Kai was one of the lucky ones. She got one. It was probably one of the best sporting events in Coos Bay and Marshfield High School history. We all left satisfied. However, the next day; we all had got the news. Pre had died in a car crash, just hours after he had beat Frank Shorter at a race in Eugene. He was just 24 years old. It was indeed a pleasure to watch him run.

Dick Butkus

I met Dick Butkus in Sacramento at the Field of Dreams. Mr. Butkus was promoting a plaster copy of his handprint on a board with a card showing one of his ferocious tackles. He was a middle linebacker for the Chicago Bears, an All-pro for many seasons. He was signing a promo of his product. He was very cordial, a nice guy. I have mine behind glass.

I met Dick Butkus, nice guy! Bobby Hurly was another guy I met. He was just getting started with the Sacramento Kings. He seemed very quiet at the time. Now he is very vocal as head coach of the Arizona State Sun Devils (ASU). I ended up watching Kane's place for him as he went up North. During that time, I took in a Football game. It was the final preseason game that year, the Seattle Seahawks versus the San Francisco 49ers. I had a perfect ticket, two rows up on the forty-yard line. I came early and put on my freezer suit due to the cold and wind. The game was played in Candlestick park stadium. I saw Jerry Rice trotting on the field like a stallion. Everybody warmed up with drills until the National Anthem and coin toss. The starters played the first half of the game: Steve Young, John Taylor, Rickey Watters, and George Siefert, coach. The Seahawks had Rick Mirrer, Cortez Kennedy, and Tom Flores, coach. The game was good. It ended 49ers over the Seahawks 13 to 9. By the way, that 49er team ended up winning the Super Bowl that Season!

Movie Idols

Actors, my favorite actor is the late Charles Bronson. His movies include some all-time favorites, like Death Wish and the Magnificent 7. I liked Hard Times. He was tough. Marlon Brando did the classic. On the Waterfront, the ultimate ageless Longshoreman movie. The Godfather was another classic. My favorite actress is Sandra Bullock, a natural beauty to me. Her movie, Blindside, was excellent.

Brandon Roy

I was at the Downtown AT&T store in Portland trying to purchase a new phone. Sarah, the sales associate said to me, "Guess who just walked in the door?" Of course, I didn't know. I was facing her. I asked, "Who?" She said, "Brandon Roy," an all-pro basketball player for the Portland Trailblazers. I told Sarah that I was going to walk up to Brandon and ask him if he would have a photo taken with me on my new phone. She agreed. So, I walked up to Brandon, told him my name, and what I wanted to do. He said, "OK." We posed and Sarah took the picture. That picture is framed. It is one of my favorite pieces of memorabilia. What nice guy!

Clint Eastwood

The Bandon Dunes Golf Course, just outside of the town of Bandon, is beautiful, at least that is what I hear. I went there early one summer evening hoping to hit some balls on the driving range. I had a group tournament at Pumpkin Ridge Golf Course for the University of Oregon, later in the week. As it turned out the lady at the Dunes information booth was very nice and let me through. As I was nearing the driving range, I parked. It was getting dark now. By my car was this tall man lighting up a cigarette. I walked up to him, and said you look like someone I know. He asked, "Who?" I replied, "Dirty Harry." He said, "I'm not him." We shook hands and I left. He most definitely wasn't Dirty Harry. But he most definitely might have been Clint Eastwood.

Ted Turner

When at the University of Idaho, I missed a symposium I wanted to attend. As luck would have it, this same symposium was being held at Washington State University. It was a symposium honoring Ted Turner with the Edward Murrow award. Ted was an adequate speaker, talking of his beginnings up to CNN news network. It was interesting.

A Life Well Lived

I have a life that has given me happiness – good friends, good family, and my passions for sports and art. It has been an interesting journey, a unique journey and one where I had many moments of pure joy.

Food

Do you like food? I used to be an eating machine until Diabetes II caught up with me. When at home in Coos Bay, mom prepared excellent meals. I learned to cook on the Kodiak fishing vessel. I practiced with fresh halibut in a Krusteaz batter, mouthwatering. Along with that we had vegetables, beans, corn, and rice pilaf. That was one meal. Other times we would pull up to a crab pot, boil some huge Dungeness and eat it.

Going out in the wild and picking edible mushrooms was a great hobby -. Our first adventure was for the common "nutty tasting" Chanterelles, delicious in spaghetti sauce, gravies, thick creamy soups, and many more applications of food. Our family could pick enough to fill a five-gallon barrel right after a good rain. Mushroom hunting in the woods was great.

Another tasty fungus, that is really hard to find, is the cauliflower mushroom. When cleaned and cooked in butter it has a good texture and tastes like clams. If you like those, lobster mushrooms, cooked in butter, are also good - like meat good with rice, or potatoes. Matsutake, or pine mushrooms, are found in the dunes around the pine trees. This mushroom has a distinct smell, not altogether unpleasant. In Japan small bits of this fungus are supposedly used as an aphrodisiac. Mushroom picking is fun. But I must warn you. Know your mushrooms; if you don't go with someone who does or else you might be waiting on a new liver. It better arrive soon too!

Some of the weirdest exotic foods I had eaten - sea turtle meat when it was legal to spear them in Hawaii, thick white slabs of meat that had a sort of sweet taste if I remember right. I thought it was even better than halibut or sturgeon. I had frog legs in a French restaurant with my wife - nine legs wrapped in lettuce. I expected small little things. They turned out to be as big as drumsticks cooked in a tempura batter. They were excellent. They had the consistency of fish, and chicken. A different type of meat that was tough but good was alligator meat. This meat was cut into strips and deep fried, heavily seasoned with a wild Cajun mix. Kangaroo jerky that was plenty tough too.

Our family and my girlfriend, who is now my wife, were having breakfast at a Restaurant in the Hawthorne District. We were all conversing. She brought up the fact

Klaus, with cigar, and friend Kenny.   Kane and Klaus.

that she had bought me a cigar in Bend. Dad had a look of fury. Suddenly my brother Kane interjected with, "You smoke Ceegah!" loudly. So, then everybody just laughed. We finished our breakfast. Yes, I like cigars. They're relaxing and help me think.

Voting

I realize that being able to vote is a privilege. I consider myself a Moderate Democrat. Supposedly today, as Democrats we are the working middle class. I think our party is weak now. Please, correct me if I'm wrong. I'm just saying that's "my opinion". As far as voter apathy, there's too much of it. If you don't like Ms. Clinton, and you don't like Trump, don't vote for either. There's plenty to vote for on that election ballot. Just Vote! Again, just voicing my opinion.

A little history lesson: Our seventh President of the United States was Andrew Jackson. He killed Indians and owned a plantation with slaves. He was our first Democrat. A military man he knew no less.

History, or Bullshit, you decide. As far as a man who started and created during real tough times, it was Franklin Delano Roosevelt (FDR), again a Democrat, who had Social Security started within his administration. His insight to see so far ahead - with jobs and infrastructure - was incredible. He was in office for three terms, I think. He was either popular or we needed him. Harry Bridges had that same type of insight. Old Abraham Lincoln ended up getting shot in the head while enjoying a show at the White house. Ole Abe lived through most of the Civil War, which still exists, even in little bits and pieces today. The prejudice, racism, and bigotry continue all over. Once again, just my opinion. Let's face it, if you are a politician. You should probably have your facts straight. Or now, if you're rich enough, just blatantly lie. Both parties do it! Whatever happened to the "Honest" factor?

Challenges

I guess my story would not be complete unless I talked about my disease afflictions. The main one is my bi-polar disorder. Call it what you will, manic-depression, "whatever", I tend to stay on the high side now, rather than get deeply depressed. This has also happened in the past. I had to be hospitalized for a week or two when the manic side had kept me up for a week straight without sleep. I tend to go crazy! It was after my homeless episode where I finally, grudgingly took to heart that I had a mental problem. It took a long time to diagnose. I am very fortunate. My wife regulates my medications. I have to take a handful of pills every evening. I'm fine. I'd like to think that I'm quite positive most of the time.

I am inflicted with Diabetes II, a royal pain in the ass. I also now have small bouts with Parkinson's disease. Sometimes I feel all that shaking helps my artwork.

When I was younger, and in high school, and college I don't remember having those full-blown side effects. It has taken a total of 20 years to make this somewhat right. Dammit, I'm still not perfect!

Friends

You better believe that there were and are people in my life who have helped me improve myself in life and competition.

Louella Aina – my Hawaiian Aunty who is probably one of the greatest female athletes ever on the Hawaiian Islands. She was always there when she was needed.

Dick Asai - We went crabbing and fishing with Dick Asai. He provided for a few families by giving Crab, perch filets, clams, mushrooms, and any assortment of berries to families. Yes, he was a provider. His downfall was he couldn't hold his alcohol. One day, I heard that Dick went fishing caught many fish. He dragged the boat in and laid down by the boat in the sand and died in his best clothes. Dick knew it was his time. Mako Hirato found Dick and took care of him. His Ceremony of life and grave of his cremated bones in the sand by the ocean will always be remembered by those who were there. Dick once told me he was just a bum. Nothing could have been further from the truth. An Oregon State graduate, he became a Professor of Chemistry and taught at Arizona State. That was all I knew about him. Other than that, he was with dad at many of my sporting events, also Kane's events too.

The Bailey family -Kenny's step-father and mother, the Baileys, are very special to me. They treat me like a part of the family. They love and care for me wholeheartedly. Thankyou Spike and Lorraine!

Bruce Bertrand – Jr. High Track coach who watched me run like the wind. Good teacher too!

Chuck Crandall - High School math teacher and coach who was so encouraging and motivational.

Les Engles – Great teacher, coach, everything.

Bill Kanui, Sr. – Aikido master, Longshoreman (deceased) who taught me a one-hour breathing technique to relax. This enabled me to win a spot on the traveling squad. My hand was raised once, as a first team Duck. Good enough for me.

The Loftus family -The Loftus family, we met by having Don Loftus tune our antique piano. Soon there were family functions. Thanksgiving was always a welcoming place at the Loftus house. There was Don, Mitzi (Dick Asai's sister) and their sons. David, Kenneth, and, Toby. The family would often run race events, and track. David, Kenneth, and Toby are totally fluent in musical instruments, music, and dance – outstanding.

Yosh Machida (deceased) – much like an uncle to me. Similar to Mr. Myagi.

Carolyn Matthews – a special lady, no nonsense. She helped me through a rough time.

Brian Milford - a friend who has collected my artwork over the recent years be it great, good, or average. A great guy! His parents are nice too- Doris and Ed.

Brian with a compound bow.   Kane & Brian at my wedding.

<u>Stan Soloman</u> (deceased) who never got the full potential out of me or Kane in Track and Field knowing that if he had us for four years each – watch out!

<u>Pete and Margaret Ward</u> – Just like another family, so welcoming and receptive!

My Union Comrades

I love my union. In so many stages of my life, the union supported me. I would not be where I am today without my union.

I want solidarity to thrive within the union. It is essential. Solidarity in definition means union. I wish my brothers well in working through the challenges they are facing today so they can be there for each other and those who have already retired.

My Immediate Family

I have been with my wife, Janet, for over ten years. I have two step-daughters and two grand-daughters and I am content.

Janet and I married on Oct. 26, 2013

Made in the USA
Las Vegas, NV
06 November 2021